IT'S ALL ABOUT THE **BOOKS**

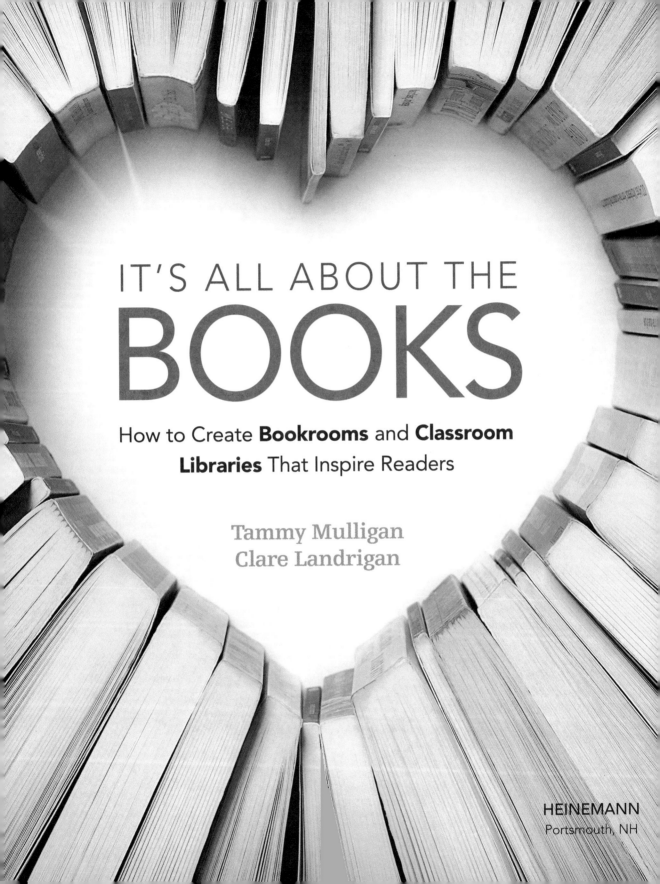

IT'S ALL ABOUT THE
BOOKS

How to Create **Bookrooms** and **Classroom** **Libraries** That Inspire Readers

Tammy Mulligan
Clare Landrigan

HEINEMANN
Portsmouth, NH

Heinemann

361 Hanover Street

Portsmouth, NH 03801–3912

www.heinemann.com

Offices and agents throughout the world

The authors and publisher wish to thank those who have generously given permission to reprint borrowed material:

Figure 2.2: From *The Construction Zone: Building Scaffolds for Readers and Writers* by Terry Thompson. Copyright © 2015 by Terry Thompson. Reproduced by permission of Stenhouse Publishers. www.stenhouse.com.

Cataloging-in-Publication Data is on file at the Library of Congress.
ISBN: 978-0-325-09813-5

Editor: Zoë Ryder White
Production: Hilary Goff
Cover and interior designs: Suzanne Heiser
Cover image: © Getty Images / David Malan
Typesetter: Valerie Levy, Drawing Board Studios LLC
Manufacturing: Steve Bernier

Printed in the United States of America on acid-free paper
22 21 20 19 18 VP 1 2 3 4 5

We dedicate this book to

The authors and illustrators of children's literature,

teachers,

school librarians,

and all the readers who give us the privilege of

connecting with them through books . . .

without you this book would not be possible.

Thank you for teaching us and inspiring us.

Contents

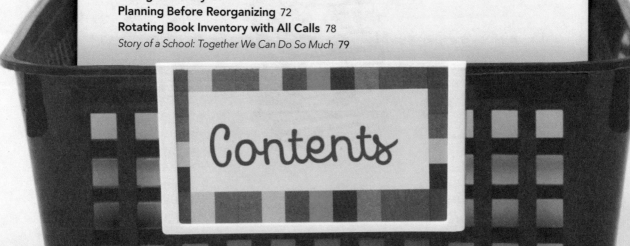

Contents

Online Resources

 To access the online resources, visit **http://hein.pub/ItsAllAboutTheBooks-login**. Enter your email address and password (or click "Create an Account" to set up an account). Once you have logged in, enter keycode **BOOKS2018** and click "Register."

FOREWORD

JENNIFER SERRAVALLO

From Tulsa to Tallahassee, Greenwood to Great Neck, Los Angeles to Louisiana, I'm often asked: How can we make sure all of our students become skilled, engaged readers? When I visit Ohio, there's conversation about the "Third Grade Guarantee"; in Marin County it's the "Third Grade Promise": All kids must be reading at or beyond the proficient level by the middle of elementary school. In many of the diverse districts in which I work, administrators are rightly concerned about achievement gaps based on income level, race, English language proficiency, etc. In many cases, districts scramble for a "fix" that will help all the problems go away. Some purchase costly computerized progress-monitoring software. Others spend a fortune on programs and kits, and the snazziest technology.

But what if the solution was simpler—less flashy, but so much more exciting? It is.

Schools need books and skilled, passionate teachers who know how to put those books into the hands of readers and help them to engage with meaningful reading. When Tammy and Clare begin consulting work in new schools, they find themselves saying: "Fire us and buy books," because they know that access to an inclusive collection of high quality books and texts that students can and want to read is one of the most significant equity issues schools face.

I've consulted in districts where many parents don't have a car, or who work multiple jobs, and physically can't get to the town's library. I taught in a school where undocumented parents were afraid to provide personal information needed to get a library card for themselves or their children. I've lived in towns where budget cuts meant shutting library doors except for a very few hours each week, and where school librarian positions were eliminated. I know for a fact that most bookstores don't carry the kinds of predictable texts our emergent readers need in kindergarten and early first grade, and even if parents can afford to purchase them, they aren't available. Schools must provide books for in-school and at-home reading.

Do the math: If a second-grader reads for a half hour or more each day in school and more at home, and it takes that student about an hour to finish a book, that means that one student will go through a stack of books each week. Multiply that stack by hundreds of students in the school and it soon becomes clear that schools need a lot of books. And not just any books—good ones. And then once they start arriving at the school, we need to organize them. And make sure kids are finding the right ones. And, and, and....

Never fear—Tammy and Clare to the rescue! This book will help you stock your school with books, on a budget—no matter what your school's budget is. Unless you have thousands of books in every classroom; a well-stocked school library; a bookroom where books are in constant circulation and not just collecting dust; a school full of children who all know how to choose books they'll love; teachers who know how to set up and organize their libraries so it suits their class, you need to hear their advice. Tammy and Clare offer us endless insider tips to make every dollar count, make the most use of digital resources available, and help teachers manage the huge job of what to do with the books once they arrive.

This book is practical, but it's also inspirational. It's clear that kids are at the heart of everything Tammy and Clare do and the pages brim with student voices: their worries, their excitement, their stories about how they are building reading lives and sharing books with others. It's also filled with teachers: we listen in as teachers interact with students around books, make recommendations, encourage students as they talk about their wishes and goals for themselves as readers, and guide them to find the books they'll love.

In this book, Tammy and Clare show us that classroom libraries and bookrooms are more than just storage places—they should be dynamic and kinetic. They show us that books are more than materials—they are the lifeblood of our classrooms.

Tammy and Clare have given us a book about books. What could be better?

ACKNOWLEDGMENTS

Like the cosmos, like cell division, like the never-ending waves
of the oceans, our readers change and grow. To study them
like scientists and to read them closely means to appreciate
this. No—to marvel at it, revel in it, and explore.

—JENNIFER SERRAVALLO

Where to begin . . . we stand on some big shoulders!

We want to thank the teachers, administrators, coaches, and students we collaborate with in our partner schools (you know who you are) for your support, flexibility, humor, warmth, and dedication to lifelong learning. Your voices are woven throughout this book—we hope you hear them.

A special shout-out to the staff of North Brookfield Elementary School, especially Linda Ahearn, Renee Buzzell, Monique Dubuc, Betsy Gorey, Andrea Maher, Melanie McGarry, Robin Pratt, Sarah Priestley, Kristin Pupecki, Becky Simpson, Tricia Tarentino, and Eric Glazier. You gave us a professional home in which to experiment, play, and learn. Thank you for allowing us to use your bookroom as our mentor and for welcoming us with a photography crew during the first week of school! Michael Shelburne, not many teachers would let the two of us loose in their classroom libraries. You inspired us with your questions, reflections, and drive to move beyond levels to engage your young readers. We cannot thank you enough.

To our colleagues and past students at the Eliot-Pearson Children's School and the Department of Child Study and Human Development, our journey together began with you, and your teachings are at the core of our educational beliefs. Your dedication to serving children and commitment to pursuing equity and justice ground us in our daily work. The Children's School was the home of our first classroom library and where we fell in love with bringing children and books together.

We are thankful to have a strong professional learning network. These folks push our thinking, engage our curiosity, and keep us laughing.

To Franki Sibberson, thank you for being our best cheerleader and once again being the first to say, "You girls should write a book about this topic!"

To Jennifer Allen, you are our go-to sounding board every time. We appreciate the endless hours you spent talking through early drafts and convincing us not to give up on the idea; thank you.

To Lynne Dorfman and Rose Cappelli, for encouraging us to write another book and keeping us laughing through the process. We are so grateful we connected with you both—your friendship means the world to us.

To Terry Thompson, for reminding us to "write what [we're] passionate about or get passionate about what [we're] writing." You helped us find our voice and got us back on track; thank you.

We cannot begin to thank the readers of our blog, Perspectives, and our virtual learning community enough. You fuel us with your questions, comments, posts, and responses. We never imagined learning could be so powerful. We want to give a shout-out to our #IMWAYR, #SOL, and #titletalk communities; writing with you helped us shape this book.

We consider ourselves blessed to have Brenda Power in our lives. Brenda, you are truly a gift. Your mentorship and friendship are priceless. You are the first person we call for advice and we know the conversation will always end with perspective and a good laugh. We are truly overwhelmed by your wisdom and continued generosity.

A huge shout-out to Jennifer Serravallo! Thank you for taking the time to listen and for believing in us—without you this book would not have been possible.

Thank you to the Heinemann team; you have made this process a joy. Sarah Fournier, thank you for holding us all together and doing the legwork to make our dream of connecting our book with the Book Love Foundation come true! Amanda Bondi, you eased the process by keeping us all on the same page. Michael Grover and Dennis Doyle, thank you for capturing our love of books and passion for reading with teachers and students through your photography. Suzanne Heiser, Sherry Day, and Elizabeth Silvis, you made our book accessible and beautiful—we love it. Hilary Goff, thanks for being the magician behind the scenes who made the process seamless and painless. To all of you, we are so grateful. Your energy, confidence, and belief in this project have been both humbling and motivating.

And to our editor, Zoë Ryder White, thank you for taking a chance on us. We hit the editor jackpot. You are truly a treasure! You embraced our crazy process and adapted to our schedule. We loved that you were always first and foremost our reader. Your authentic response always proved energizing and insightful. You listened when we needed to talk, allowed us to get messy, and guided us when we were feeling lost. You helped us grow our thinking and discover the heart of this book.

Our heartfelt thanks to Penny Kittle for her vision and dedication to the belief that every child needs access to books. We will be forever grateful to you for giving us the opportunity to bring children and books together by accepting the royalties of this book as a donation to the Book Love Foundation.

And finally, we thank our families. You continue to support us in our work and passion for literacy. You are never surprised by our newest idea and are always willing to help us when we get in over our heads. We know we have missed some games and shows; ordered takeout more often than we would have liked; and spent what should have been family time working on this project. Writing this book was a sacrifice for everyone, but your reaction when we told you about Book Love and the impact this book will have on kids made it all worthwhile. Thank you for reminding us what really matters in the great scheme of things. We love you!

1

What Does It Take to Develop Lifelong Readers? Research Says . . . Books

By putting a book into the hands of a child, we can put hope directly into that child's hands. We can put love directly into that child's hands and we can show them, look: you have the power to make this world better.

—MR. SCHU (JOHN SCHUMACHER)

Story of a Reader: Creating a Community of Readers

Kim, a third-grade teacher, schedules one group of readers to refresh their independent reading books each day. As the Tuesday group is choosing books in the classroom library, she notices they are deep in conversation and walks over to listen in.

"Hey, didn't you read this series last month? What did you think of it?" one reader asks a friend.

"I liked it, but I don't like twists and turns in the plot. You do, so this might not be the book for you."

Another reader chimes in, "Have you read the Secrets of Droon series? This one is nonstop twists and turns–you will love it."

"Let me check it out. I've never heard of it," the first replies.

Another student comments, "I just finished the Fairy Realm series. I have no idea what to read next."

"What are you in the mood for?" a friend asks.

"Well, we're supposed to choose one graphic novel for our small group this month. Maybe I'll start with picking some of those."

The student peruses the options for a few minutes and then signals the others. "Come check out these graphic novels! *Hilo* and *Dog Man* look awesome, and they are both a series. I can't wait for our small group to meet." (See Figure 1.1.)

Figure 1.1 Students discuss book options for their small group.

We couldn't help but notice that in this classroom, selecting books is about being part of a reading community. The readers seem to know each other's preferences and what books to recommend. We wondered how Kim set this time up in her classroom. How did she decide who would "refresh" together? Did she highlight particular baskets of books, or could they choose from any basket in the classroom library?

We were not surprised to hear that Kim had thoughtfully created the conditions that made the interactions between these students possible. It's clear that she thinks deeply about her classroom library to ensure she has the books she needs to help her students develop reading habits for a lifetime and to support instruction. It is also clear she has a classroom library with a wide variety and quantity of books.

Research Demonstrates
That Books Matter

Research demonstrates again and again that access to an abundant supply of books in school and classroom libraries increases both motivation and reading achievement. Numerous national and international studies have linked the number of books in a school to standardized test achievement (Sinclair-Tarr and Tarr 2007), cognitive ability, and reading comprehension test scores (Krashen 2004, McQuillan 1998).

The National Council of Teachers of English 2017 position statement on classroom libraries (see www.ncte.org/positions/statements/classroom-libraries) synthesized decades of research highlighting the importance of classroom libraries. "Classroom libraries—physical or virtual—play a key role in providing access to books and promoting literacy; they have the potential to increase student motivation, engagement, and achievement and help students become critical thinkers, analytical readers, and informed citizens. We know that no book is right for every student, and classroom libraries offer ongoing opportunities for teachers to work with students as individuals to find books that will ignite their love for learning, calm their fears, answer their questions, and improve their lives in any of the multiple ways only literature can" (NCTE 2017, 1).

But how many books do we need to get these results? Fountas and Pinnell's research (1996) suggests that teachers need between three hundred and six hundred titles in their classroom library. The International Reading Association (1999) recommends that schools need to have at least seven books per student, and the American Library Association (Hack, Hepler, and Hickman 1993) suggests three hundred titles in a classroom library with supplements from a well-stocked school library (Neuman 2005). In 2017, Lucy Calkins wrote on the Teachers College Reading and Writing Project website that "a general rule of thumb when provisioning for libraries is about 30 books per child as a starting point. This is a starting point; most schools are regularly adding to classroom libraries in order to guarantee that students have ample reading material." Kelly Gallagher suggests "that nothing less than a classroom book flood will suffice—not 200 titles but 2,000" (2009, 53).

There is also wide and documented research supporting the need for *student-selected* reading: "Students read more, understand more, and are more likely to continue reading when they have the opportunity to choose what they read. In a 2004 meta-analysis, Guthrie and Humenick found that the two most powerful instructional design factors for improving reading motivation and comprehension were (1) student access to many books and (2) personal choice of what to read" (Allington and Gabriel 2012).

Research has also linked book access to student reading identity. Students with access to books and the opportunity to choose the books they read develop habits of lifelong learning and curiosity. They are more likely to go to college and to succeed in the workforce. Choice and independence have also been shown to positively impact strategic learning behaviors (Ivey and Johnston 2013, 273). The 2007 National Endowment for the Arts report *To Read or Not to Read* determined that "regular reading not only boosts the likelihood of an individual's academic and economic success—facts that are not especially surprising—but it also seems to awaken a person's social and civic sense" (Lyengar and Giola 2007, 6).

While access to books is important for all of our students, it has proven critical for our students from low-income households, many of whom do not have equal access to books in or out of school. Studies have shown that school and classroom libraries in underserved communities have fewer books (Krashen 1997). If we want to take steps toward closing the achievement gap, providing access to books in schools is a good place to start. Cunningham and Allington assert, "While we would love to wave a magic wand and transform the homes of all children into literacy-rich environments, this is not within our power. What is within our power is the ability to create literacy-rich environments within our schools" (1999, 22).

Our own experience in schools reflects these findings. When we begin work with our partner schools, in most cases, book volume does not even come close to what is recommended. In schools with a high percentage of students living in poverty, the numbers tend to be far worse. In the few classrooms that do have sufficient books, it is often due to the personal financing of the classroom teachers. If we know the importance of books for both academic and economic achievement, is it right to expect teachers to personally fund and supply their own classroom libraries? Allington has the same question: "It has long puzzled me why the adequacy of school libraries and classroom book collections are not a key topic in teacher labor agreement negotiations" (2000, 60). Books are key instructional tools. Schools need to prioritize the funding of purchasing books so all students can access the tools they need to be successful.

How to Get the Books We Need in Schools

We have been partnering with school districts as literacy consultants for the past fifteen years. We find that 90 percent of the time, when asked by a superintendent what he or she should do to get the desired academic results, we reply: "Fire us and buy some books." We find again and again that teachers do not have the tools they need to bring the research on literacy best practices to life. Richard Allington's research (2002) on the essential components of effective literacy instruction identified the following:

1. Increase actual reading activity.

2. Select more appropriate literacy texts.

3. Enhance useful strategy instruction.

If we build the structures and develop the curriculum for this work to happen, but do not have a wide variety of books for the students to read, it fails. Books matter—we cannot teach literacy without authentic literature. "If the goal is to support growth in reading, there are few decisions that will have more payoff than the decision to give students access to high-quality and high-interest fiction and nonfiction" (Calkins, Mallaney, and Frazin 2016, 5).

We want to share what we have learned over the years on how to bring this research to life on a budget. We have been revising classroom libraries and school bookrooms with teachers and administrators for more than a decade and have learned many lessons along the way.

We think of each classroom library as a hub of literacy for all students and a bookroom as an annex to every classroom library. This is how we can make each teacher's book supply endless—or at least *seem* endless in the eyes of a reader. We now design each space with the other in mind. In this book, we will share the process we use to design classroom libraries so they work seamlessly with school bookrooms and how we design bookrooms to make it easy for teachers to find books to engage and scaffold all students in the school community.

Overview of This Book

Getting started with provisioning and designing classroom libraries and bookrooms to support lifelong readers involves collaboration, planning, and some elbow grease! We organized this book to walk you through a step-by-step process of how to get more bang for your books. From design, to inventory, to purchasing, organizing, and using these books in the classroom, we will show you how to make the most of what you have and how to get what you need on a budget. We'll bring you into classrooms and invite you to join teacher planning sessions to show how we use the organization of the books to enhance instruction and engage students.

Each chapter includes photos, resources, booklists, and a step-by-step outline of the process so you can start tomorrow. We know there are authors, illustrators, publishers, and resources we did not include in this book and, for this, we apologize. It would be impossible to include every book we love, and we continue to be introduced to books each day. Our intention is to honor all children's book authors and illustrators—mentioned and unmentioned—in this book. We hope the variety of examples we share will provide the right balance of guidance and flexibility so the design you create reflects your vision and passions. It's a book about books—what could be better than that?

Here's what to expect from the next chapters.

CHAPTER 2:
Choosing and Using Books: The Heart and Soul of Literacy

In this chapter we discuss the role of books as both instructional tools and the vehicles to support the development of the identity and habits of a reader. We share our thoughts on text complexity, directly address the controversy over leveling texts, and show how to strike a balance that supports students' reading identities.

CHAPTER 3:
Designing Classroom Libraries and Bookrooms to Work Together: Maximizing Access

In Chapter 3, we take you on a tour of classroom libraries and bookrooms so you can see firsthand how to design each with the other in mind. We share many different ways to create a bookroom—including when your school doesn't have an actual *room* for the bookroom. We share different models for collaboration, and we explain how the design of bookrooms and classroom libraries can support both the instructional needs of a teacher and the desires of a reader. We show how to design classroom libraries and bookrooms so they work seamlessly with each other to provide a seemingly endless supply of books.

CHAPTER 4:
What Books Do You Have? What Books Do You Need?
The Inventory Process
In this chapter, we provide an inventory process that will help you take stock of what you have and identify what you need. This process will teach you some ways to collaborate and get organized so that you can plan for and prioritize purchasing as well as reorganization.

CHAPTER 5:
More Bang for Your Books: Provisioning Your School with Books
We are thrifty shoppers. We know budgets are tight and teachers often spend personal funds to provision their classroom libraries. In this chapter we share all we have learned about ways to enhance your school's book collection on a budget, as well as our favorite tried-and-true time-saving tips and cautions. We will be with you every step of the way, sharing sample booklists, order forms, publisher hyperlinks, sample budgets, and sample order guides.

CHAPTER 6:
So Many Books . . . How Does a Reader Choose? Supporting
Readers' Choice and Agency with Books
The sooner we involve our students in the process of organizing the books—in both the classroom and the bookroom—the sooner they will be on their way to developing the habits and dispositions of a reader. In this chapter, we show how we can use book organization to help students find the right book at the right time in order to meet their goals and develop their reading identities.

CHAPTER 7:
Got Books . . . Now What? Organizing Books to Support Instruction
Chapter 6 describes how to organize books in support of student choice, and this chapter shows how to organize books in support of instructional goals. We peek into grade-level team meetings and see how teachers use books to plan.

We take a closer look at the baskets in classroom libraries and bookrooms to see how teachers use books to support curriculum and student engagement. We even show you some suggested titles in these baskets and give some tips for how we use them to scaffold instruction.

CHAPTER 8:

Digital Resources: Opening a World of Possibilities

Digital resources have the potential to dramatically impact access to texts for students. In this chapter we share how we use the ever-evolving world of digital resources to increase access, engage students, and enhance our instruction. We invite you into classrooms to see how we use some of our favorite digital resources. Finally, we show how we are integrating digital resources into classroom libraries and bookrooms to create text sets that increase volume and choice.

Story of a School: Celebrating a Community of Readers

Spaulding Elementary School spent a year getting books into the hands of its readers. Staff members shared books, reorganized books, and purchased books. Teachers spent time designing classroom libraries and creating a new bookroom. In June we surveyed teachers and students to hear their thoughts and reflections about reading over the past year. Here are some things we heard from teachers:

"We have a waiting list for the books we borrowed from the bookroom!"

"I know my students so much better as readers–better than I ever have before."

"I love that my students are talking about books and authors. There is a buzz in my room around reading."

"I see less 'fake' or compliant reading. Students are really engaged in their reading."

"Some students are seeing themselves as readers for the first time."

"Students are talking to each other about the books they are reading."

"Students love to read. It feels different."

Here are some things we heard from students:

"I love reading workshop. It is so much fun to read books that my friends are reading."

"I want to read books that I can read easily so I can understand better. I used to just want to read long, hard books. Now I have so many options; I choose books for different reasons."

"We had to go on a field trip this week. I was so upset that we had to miss our reading time."

"I have a plan for my reading. I read at home and at school. I know what I like to read."

We witnessed a celebration of books and reading throughout the school. Teachers noticed that for the first time students were talking about books socially, that students' accuracy and comprehension improved, and that they knew their students better as readers. Students said they got to know authors and series in a way they never had in the past. This school's story brings the research to life: if students read more–more texts they choose and can read meaningfully–they will become lifelong readers.

2

Choosing and Using Books
The Heart and Soul of Literacy

Dreams lurk in books. We must never forget that. We have been given the privilege of this life in teaching. Let us have the strength to start where they are and lead them.

—PENNY KITTLE

Story of a Reader: A Reader's Identity Is More Than a Level

Sam is using the books in his independent reading bag to build a tower. As he sees us walking over, he quickly takes it down, knowing he should be reading. When we ask him about it, he responds, "Well, there are no shark books in the F basket. I love sharks. I want to learn about sharks, but I can't read the books in the H basket."

Sam's story is a common one. He spent the first half of the year in a structured intervention program so his experience with choosing books was limited. He identifies more with his reading level than his interests. We want Sam to know readers consider both interest *and* accessibility when choosing books. "Let's take a look in the classroom library to see what we can find," we suggest. We grab two baskets—Ocean Animals and Predators.

We ask, "Are you interested only in sharks or all ocean animals or predators?"

Sam wonders, "Predators? What's a predator?"

"It's an animal that hunts other animals."

He leans in. "That sounds cool! Do we have any of those books?"

"We do, in this basket. And we have some shark books in this basket."

Sam shifts backward ever so slightly. "Can I take books from these baskets?" What he's really asking, of course, is if there are any books that he can comfortably read in the baskets. Sam *wants* to be an engaged reader. He wants to find books about a topic he loves that he can also read in a meaningful way.

"Why don't you take a look and see if there are any books that would be a good match?"

Sam digs in and then turns and says, "Thanks. I want to be a marine biologist, so these books will help me!"

As noted in Chapter 1, research shows that access to books matters for reading achievement, and our experience tells us that we need more than volume to create lifelong readers. We also need to empower teachers to spark and fuel the love of reading in their students. It is great Sam chooses books he can read. But we want him to have access to books that he can read *and* that engage him. At the beginning of the conference, Sam was using book level as his only lens for choosing books. This isn't uncommon, especially with emergent readers. Our job is to help them understand that looking through all the options within an instructional range is just *one* way readers choose books. Another way is to look through books on a topic that interests them and then find one within their instructional range.

Figure 2.1 lists several bodies of research that support the importance of readers considering both engagement and accuracy when choosing books.

It is important for students to have lots of opportunities to access easy-to-read texts of their choosing. When students read at an independent level, they comprehend deeply, connect authentically, and share their thinking with other readers. When students sit in front of frustration-level text all day every day, they are not developing into strategic, engaged, joyful readers. Similarly, when we ignore readers' preferences, interests, and goals, we hinder their growth and habits. We need to support the research on both engagement and accuracy to develop lifelong readers.

The term *lifelong reader* is more than a slogan or jargon in a mission statement. Lifelong readers need passion, agency, and a sense of inquiry in their reading

Where's The Balance?

Engagement	Accuracy
Researchers agree that engagement is essential to helping children become strong readers. When students are engaged in reading, they are able to self-generate learning opportunities (Guthrie and Wigfield 1997). Allington (2000), a researcher concerned with what matters most when working with struggling readers, writes that engagement in reading has been found to be the most powerful instructional activity for fostering reading growth.	Good readers read with accuracy almost all of the time. The last sixty years of research on optimal text difficulty—a body of research that began with Betts (1946)—consistently demonstrates the importance of having students read texts they can read accurately and understand. In fact, research shows that reading at 98 percent or higher accuracy is essential for reading acceleration. Anything less slows the rate of improvement, and anything below 90 percent accuracy doesn't improve reading ability at all (Allington and Gabriel 2012; Ehri, Dreyer, Flugman, and Gross 2007).

Figure 2.1: Where's the Balance?

lives. A person who reads for a lifetime is a person who is engaged in all aspects of his life. He needs to have a disposition for learning, connecting, responding, and taking action. Students also need to read with accuracy and comprehension. They need to learn how to decode effectively and efficiently. They need to be active, metacognitive, proficient readers. Becoming a lifelong reader requires both skills and habits. *Books* are our tools to develop lifelong readers. The only way to merge true choice and accessibility is to have *options*—and lots of them!

What Do Readers Consider When Choosing Books?

When we think about how to teach students to choose books, we start by thinking about ourselves as readers. What do we think about when we choose books? We most often think about the factors that make up our reading identities, such as our

- community
- interests and preferences
- projects and inquiry
- habits and dispositions
- life events
- goals.

It is critical that the books we have in schools and in classrooms keep a reader's identity in mind. Research has shown that students rank classrooms last as a source for finding interesting reading materials (Worthy, Moorman, and Turner 1999). We want students to be able to find books they love at school so that we can build their dispositions as readers as we teach them *how* to read. Our classrooms need to be provisioned with a range of books so every student has the opportunity to set meaningful goals and to work to achieve those goals with books that engage him or her.

What Do Teachers Consider When Choosing Books?

While we must always honor a reader's identity and preferences, we also must keep our instructional goals in mind. Teachers often ask us, "Is it OK to tell our students what to read sometimes?" Independent reading time is sometimes confused with "free reading," reading time without teacher input. Students need to learn how to decode, comprehend, and respond to different types of texts. In order to do so they need to read these different types of texts.

We believe that readers should always have choice. However, at certain points throughout the year, you might offer choice within a selection of texts organized by author, genre, element, device, topic, or content, depending on your instructional goals. When we curate a collection of texts in this way, we honor students' preferences while also setting parameters that allow us to teach into particular goals. We are continually trying to balance our instructional goals, readers' developmental needs, and readers' preferences.

There are many factors to consider when we think about organizing books to support our instructional role in a reader's development, primarily

- our instructional model
- ELA and content curriculum standards
- text complexity.

Each of these factors impacts the others—it is impossible to think of one without considering its relationship to the others. Let's take a closer look at the interdependent relationship between them.

• Instructional Model •

The gradual release of responsibility model of instruction (Pearson and Galla-gher 1983) is the foundation of our literacy block. This model calls for instruc-tion with a high level of teacher responsibility, instruction with a shared level of responsibility between teacher and student, and instruction with a high level of student responsibility. (See Figure 2.2.) We need books for each type of instruction.

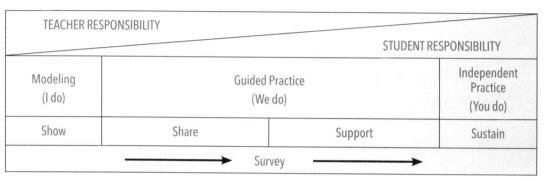

Figure 2.2: The gradual release of responsibility model, from *The Construction Zone* (Thompson 2015)

Whole-Class Lessons—High Level of Teacher Responsibility

Teachers need to quickly find not only texts that will help us teach content, but also texts to read aloud, and texts that expose students to a variety of structures, genres, and crafts during our whole-class lessons. (See Figure 2.3.) Schools need books that support instructional content and standards for each grade level and that span a range of text lengths, structures, formats, and complexity so we can meet the needs of all students.

Some books might be used for whole-class writing or reading lessons. For example, if a first-grade class is studying ellipses in writers workshop, demon-strating with books that use this craft is crucial (e.g., we might use the Crayons series by Drew Daywalt). If third graders are studying different ways authors structure texts to compare and contrast a topic, we need books to serve as models as we teach (for example, Jerry Pallotta's Who Would Win? series). Building and maintaining an organized collection of books that gives teachers easy access to what they need when they need it is critical to effective, respon-sive teaching.

Figure 2.3: Students need to be read aloud to every day.

Guided Practice—Shared Responsibility

Not every small-group lesson or experience requires multiple copies of a common text to support a shared responsibility. We generally need multiple copies of a text when we want to offer a small group of readers guided support across a book or if we want to use it in a book club.

Here are some types of books we typically want multiple copies of:

- the first book in a series
- books with a long waiting list of eager readers
- books with an unfamiliar text structure
- books that support a content area topic
- books we notice students like to read together
- books that explore thought-provoking or trending topics.

We find that having six copies of these types of books expands options for how we can use them instructionally and builds on the social power of small groups. (See Figure 2.4.)

Figure 2.4: Small groups give us a chance to listen and observe our students interact with text more closely.

Independent Practice—High Level of Student Responsibility

Students need time to independently practice and apply the strategies they are learning. We need a lot of books to support students during this time and it is essential that there are enough options for them to have choice and voice in their book selection. Donalyn Miller reminds us, "If we really want our students to become wild readers, independent of our support and oversight, sometimes the best thing we can do is get out of the way" (2014, 109). When we have enough books and organize them to support both engagement and access, it makes it easier to step aside.

• ELA and Content Curriculum Standards •

We need a range of texts that support our grade-level curriculum, both literacy standards and content standards. Teachers need books in these areas to use as models, for students to read with guided support, and for students to read independently. When we include in our libraries books that cover science and social studies standards, we give students time to build content knowledge during the literacy block, which opens up time for project-based learning and hands-on experiments and experiences during social studies and science time. Third graders studying life cycles in science, for example, will benefit from access to relevant texts they might read during the literacy block, freeing up time for a field trip to a local pond or for hatching butterflies for some action research.

• Text Complexity •

Students need access to a variety of texts within each band of text complexity. A reader's work, whether in the context of literacy, social studies, or science, is either supported or challenged by the complexity of the text she is reading. It follows that we need to provide a range of texts so that each child has access to books within the appropriate band of text complexity—books that complement the rigor of the task at hand. We need to provide opportunities for our readers to try lots of different types of books for various purposes and not view reading simply as moving up a trajectory of difficulty. Book-leveling systems are instructional tools that help teachers consider how text complexity supports readers when they are learning something new and scaffolds them as they develop independence. In elementary education, we commonly use book levels to talk about book access as related to accuracy, so levels get a lot of play in our instructional conversations.

Levels—Intent Versus Impact

When Marie Clay first created book levels, she did not intend them to be used to organize books for student selection. She defined levels as "a gradient of text that reflects a defined continuum of characteristics related to the level of support and challenge the reader is offered" (Fountas and Pinnell 2005, 9). In Clay's model, levels are an instructional tool to help us determine the types of texts that will support our readers instructionally. Each level provides some supports and some challenges. Teachers choose a text level that will offer appropriate support to scaffold the development of a reader.

Fountas and Pinnell adapted Clay's Reading Recovery levels to support the development of a typical reading progression. Their leveling system was designed to help classroom teachers select books for guided reading. Book levels were used to help teachers easily find books that would provide the appropriate amount of problem-solving opportunities for readers. At first, levels were used

While we don't want students laboring to read text that is too difficult for them to comprehend, or burn through books that provide little intellectual challenge, we must be mindful of how reading level systems affect how children see reading and themselves as readers. Reading levels are meant to guide, not limit or define children's reading choices. Consider what reading level systems offer and what they don't.

—Donalyn Miller, "On the Level" (2017, 1)

only by teachers. Even in relation to independent reading, it was never recommended to label baskets of books with a level. "Another suggestion is to organize leveled baskets of books as part of the library to scaffold students selecting appropriate books for independent reading. It is not necessary for these baskets to have level labels on them; we do not want readers to think of themselves as level D or E" (Fountas and Pinnell 1999, 13).

Over time, a leveling system designed to inform teachers morphed into the primary organizing principle in many classroom libraries. "We created the levels for books, and not as labels for children, and our goal was that these levels be in the hands of people who understand their complexity and use them to make good decisions in instruction" (Parrott 2017, 1). The idea was that if books were organized by level, students could choose books of interest from certain baskets that would support the skills and strategies they were learning. The levels on the baskets provided a scaffold when we could not be there to support our students' book selection. Win-win, right? Not so much. Over time children begin to identify themselves with the levels of books they were asked to choose—the basket label became the reader label. While this was clearly not teachers' intention, it often became the impact. Rather than simply having a basket of E books, we suddenly had kids who identified as E readers. We have to keep in mind that *we level books, not readers*. Szymusiak and Sibberson, in their groundbreaking book *Beyond Leveled Books*, reminded all of us, "If we know that our children are unique and the reading process is complex, why would we limit our ability to match children to books by relying on a leveled list created by a person or a company that doesn't know us or our children?" (2001, 15). We never want a level to exclude a reader from a type of book she wants to read. Readers need to understand that both engagement and accuracy are important to their development and we need to organize books to support both.

Where Are the Books? School Libraries, Bookrooms, and Classroom Libraries

Many schools have three types of spaces that house books: the school library, the bookroom or some other shared schoolwide storage space (closets, shelves, carts, or crates), and classroom libraries. Each serves a particular role for students and teachers.

• School Libraries •

We believe the primary role of a school library is to give students the freedom to find, choose, and read whatever they want. We do not believe school libraries are meant to be organized to support curricular or instructional goals or to supply classroom libraries with the volume of books needed. Librarians are masters of introducing students to the perfect books for their interests and the resources they need to learn at a personal level of inquiry. We would never want instructional goals to dictate how a library is organized or the access a reader has to books. The library is a place where students can explore, dream, learn, imagine, and be welcomed into the "literacy club" (Smith 1988).

The school library and librarians support teachers by keeping them apprised of new books, suggesting authors, finding resources they need to support curriculum standards, coplanning units of study, and supporting research projects. The librarian is a learning facilitator for a school—helping teachers and students gain access to, evaluate, share, and synthesize information. Research supports the importance of quality school libraries in schools. A tweet by the Stephenville High School library (April 30, 2017) quotes library science professor Teri Lesesne of Sam Houston State University saying, "There is solid research that shows the positive impact of librarians and libraries on test scores. More importantly, school libraries provide access to a world of ideas for every student" (twitter.com/search?f=tweets&q=%40professornana%20%23slm17&src=typd).

School libraries are essential. We are concerned with how school libraries are being used to source classroom libraries and the diminishing role of the librarian in many schools. If books keep shifting from the school library to classroom libraries, it puts the profession of the librarian at risk. "According to a recent survey, 39 percent of school principals nationwide reported not having a full-time librarian. 'Many schools are experiencing severe fiscal challenges. . . . That has affected many school libraries,' Librarian of Congress Carla Hayden said" (CBS News 2016). The preservation of school libraries and librarians is yet another reason we need to work together to get books into classrooms.

All the research on the volume of books we shared in Chapter 1 applies to school libraries as well. It is our hope that our education system continues to invest in school libraries and librarians, as they serve a unique and vital role in the development of lifelong readers. In the words of John Schumacher, the ambassador of school libraries for Scholastic Book Fairs, a school library "shouldn't be viewed as a privilege. It should be seen as a right. We cannot cut school libraries" (CBS News 2016). We have the utmost respect for the work and the role of the school library and librarians and see the impact each serves in our daily work. We will not, however, be further discussing the topic of school libraries in detail as the scope of this book is sourcing classroom libraries.

• Bookrooms •

A bookroom is a shared space for books in a school. We are often asked how our vision of a bookroom differs from that of a school or a classroom library. We believe a bookroom differs from a school library in that its *primary purpose* is to supply books to classroom libraries (see page 38). The bookroom is a shared instructional resource that provides teachers with a greater range of books for their readers and for their instructional goals. It is the perfect complement to a vibrant school library and a well-designed classroom library. We cannot rely on teachers to continually spend personal funds to get the tools needed to teach. We know many teachers do this, and will probably continue to do this, but we believe schools should take on some of this financial burden. (See Chapter 5 for specific ideas about funding book purchases.)

Reenvisioning how you organize books using bookrooms gives more bang for your books in terms of both time and money. Elementary readers are continually growing and changing; change is the essence of this developmental stage. Books need to be organized so we can refresh and rotate the books in our classroom libraries to meet the evolving needs and interests of our students. This provides students and teachers with more choice. The needs and interests of each classroom vary from year to year, and having baskets of books stored in a central location helps teachers find texts to engage each new class of individuals from year to year. The bookroom is an annex of sorts for each classroom library.

Ideally, bookrooms supply the depth, breadth, and volume of books to supplement what each teacher needs and what every student wants. They provide enough books at each level for students to read independently, multiple copies of texts to support small-group and partner instruction, mentor texts for whole-class lessons, whole-class texts for interactive read-alouds, and those "hot off the press" titles. All of this is organized in grab-and-go baskets for a teacher to simply (and quickly) take and incorporate into her classroom library. Classroom libraries need to stay fresh and attract readers with a flow of new books, and bookrooms allow us to make this happen.

• Classroom Libraries •

The classroom library is the home of a class' reading community. It is where readers trade books and offer suggestions. Its primary role is building a literacy community in each classroom and ensuring that each student is a member (see page 26). In the ideal world, every classroom library would be limitless! Teachers would have a budget to continually revise and add to their libraries to reflect and include

- the instructional range of learners each year
- the new standards for curriculum
- the new grade level they choose or are assigned to teach
- new books as they are published.

If books are the heart and soul of teaching literacy, then we need to make sure every classroom library has what it needs for every student. We rarely find a classroom library that is equipped to meet the needs of each student year after year. But if their primary role is to create a reading community, classroom libraries need to be flexible and responsive to the changing needs, diverse identities and ranges of interests of our students.

We remember outfitting our first classroom library with books from yard sales, our parents' attics, and closeout bookstores like Buck-a-Book. We know you most likely did the same thing. However, doctors and lawyers aren't expected to source their tools at yard sales—nor should teachers, we believe, be expected to provide their own classroom libraries. So how can we fill our rooms with the books we need to ensure each student becomes a member of the literacy club?

How can we keep our students engaged, invested, and excited about new titles throughout the year?

Working together as a school community has been the answer for us. We believe we can no longer think only about the readers in our own classrooms. We must hold ourselves accountable to every reader in every classroom in a school. Every reader deserves the opportunity to become a lifelong reader. Bookrooms make this possible for all students. Bookrooms are a practical, economical, and effective solution to making sure each teacher has the volume of books he needs for each student to become a lifelong reader, year after year. Research supports it and our hearts know it. It is no longer a question of *if* . . . now, on to the *how*!

Story of a School: Make the Best Use of the Books You Have

Murkland School had experienced many initiatives over the years. The school often used state and federal grants to purchase different programs or learn various new instructional models. When the school set a goal to have students read authentic texts daily in a workshop model, they realized the books that came with the current anthology did not meet the range of skills or preferences of the students. They needed classroom libraries.

But instead of going straight to ordering books, the teachers and administrators at Murkland decided to see what was already in the school. Over the years, the school had purchased many books for these various initiatives. As each new initiative came and went, the materials were packed away and stored. As we helped them search through the materials, we found lots of great books. Many were in multiple-copy sets, so we had to decide which to keep together for small-group instruction and which to break up into single copies for independent reading. We noticed there was more fiction than nonfiction and very few series. By taking stock of what books they already had on hand, this community realized they were already well on their way to provisioning the bookroom to supplement classroom libraries. The process also helped us prioritize what to order because we knew we needed more books for independent reading, more series, and more nonfiction titles. This school worked together to ensure every reader had access to high-quality books.

3

Designing Classroom Libraries and Bookrooms to Work Together

Maximizing Access

Design is not just what it looks like and feels like. Design is how it works.

—STEVE JOBS

Story of a Reader: You Can't Love What You Can't Read

Michael was, on the outside, a deeply engaged reader. He was partway through the third book in the Warriors series when we visited his classroom. When we noted his engagement, his teacher, Carol, said, "Yes, but the problem is, he can't actually access that text at all. He's reading that series because his older brother loves it."

After we talked with Carol, we learned that the school did have some baskets containing fantasy series in the bookroom that would be a better match for Michael in terms of complexity, and she planned to have them on hand when she conferred with him next. He was still reading the Warriors series when she approached the next day.

"So, Michael, how is it going?" Carol asked.

"Great! I love this series," he replied.

"Tell me what you love about it," Carol continued.

"What do you mean?"

"What made you choose this book?" she added.

"I don't know." Michael paused to think. "I like that everyone likes it."

"That makes sense. I love to read what other people recommend, too. Are you tied to the Warriors series, or are you willing to try a different fantasy series that other readers love?" Carol handed Michael a basket. He looked through it and pulled a book out.

"This one looks cool. The cats have wings." He paused and put it back in the basket.

"Thanks, but I think I am all set. I will stick with the Warriors series."

Carol nodded and continued, "Here's the thing. There are strategies I need to teach you that I can't teach you well with the Warriors series. During our literacy block, it's important that you choose a text that will interest you like Warriors does, but that will also support you in learning and applying the new strategies and ideas you are learning."

Michael asked, "Am I the only student who has to learn the strategies with a different book?"

"You are not. I am teaching everyone strategies during this time of day, and I need everyone to choose books that allow them to practice what I am teaching. I want you to love reading and grow as a reader. In fact, Sean and Matt are reading the Catwings series, too. Do you want to talk with them about it? I know you like taking recommendations from friends," Carol responded.

"They are? Are you sure?"

"Positive. Why don't you go ask them about it?"

He headed off, book in hand, to talk with his peers.

How many times have you encountered this scenario: a student is struggling through a book that is high-interest from a topic, genre, or series stand-point without being able to make meaning out of it? What to do? Well, choice doesn't have to mean a free-for-all, and access doesn't have to mean restriction.

We simply need to think about how we can broaden a student's understanding of how we choose books and provide choices within those categories. Rather than telling them what they cannot read, let's try showing them all the options they have to choose from.

Organizing Books for Access

When it comes to books, the word *access* has layers of meaning. As teachers, we often use this word to describe how a student interacts with the complexity of a text—does a student have the skills to read a particular text level? Access can also, of course, describe book availability in general. Both definitions are critical. In the previous vignette, Michael needed physical access to a book he would be able to intellectually access as a reader: a book he would both love and be able to read. As teachers, we need access to books that support the curriculum we need to teach and the individual students we are teaching.

Giving students choice in their reading lives does not mean we don't intervene when we see students struggling to comprehend books they've chosen. In math we do not give students full choice—they cannot choose to do algebra if they don't understand place value. Choice does not have to be a free-for-all in order to provide options, and matching students to texts does not have to be restrictive to be supportive. Choice means students have some ownership in the decision-making process. When we provide students with a range of books to choose from, we are still supporting their reading identities. When we teach them that readers make choices based on both complexity and interest, we are broadening their perspective and understanding. It is not enough to simply have a lot of books in our classrooms. We need to organize those books so teachers and students can easily access what they want when they need it.

Book organization in our classrooms impacts students' ability to access the right book at the right time. Our systems for organizing books need to be flexible to meet their evolving needs and interests. Our systems also need to be simple and responsive to our instructional needs. How can we organize our books so they are readily available to support both the development and the disposition of a reader? How can we count on finding the right book at the right moment when students' needs and interests are continually changing? How can we design our classroom libraries and bookrooms to maximize access? Read on to find out!

Studying Classroom Library Design

A picture is worth a thousand words. We like to study mentor classroom libraries before we begin designing the layout of the space we will use. What are the possibilities? What have other teachers done? How can your classroom library design complement and work seamlessly with the bookroom? Let's take a tour of some different classroom libraries to see what we can learn about the craft of classroom library design (see Figures 3.1 through 3.4).

A Guided Tour of
Classroom Library Designs

Figure 3.1: Look at the accessibility of these books for kindergarten students. The texts are placed at just the right height for young readers, and the labels on the baskets clearly display what texts students will find inside.

Figure 3.2: This third-grade classroom library is so visually appealing and accessible to readers. The labels on the bins have pictures of book covers, authors, and characters to help readers find books they love.

Figure 3.3: When readers look at this fourth-grade classroom library, they see options. These books are organized by series, genre, interest, author, and topic. We love the catchy labels this teacher uses to advertise the books as well, such as "Strong Girl Characters."

Figure 3.4: Doesn't this fifth-grade classroom library make you want to cozy up with a great book? The atmosphere is so inviting. The books are organized by author, topic, and series so readers can easily find what they are looking for or slow down and browse for a bit.

Mentor Classroom Library: Come On In!

We have chosen one classroom library to serve as a mentor as we explain the details and specifics of each section. (See Figure 3.5.) You will, of course, consider your own space and students as you DIY the classroom library that is right for you. See Figure 3.6 for an annotated graphic of our mentor library, which will show you how all of the parts make a whole.

Figure 3.5: Welcome to our mentor classroom library! As this library evolved, we focused on creating sections within the library and reorganizing the existing books to reflect the interests and preferences of this classroom's young readers.

Designing Classroom Libraries for Access

Elementary classrooms are busy places! The design of the classroom library is critical to the flow of traffic in a classroom and the tone it sets for literacy. We want the classroom library to say, "Come on in—all readers are welcome here!" Ideally we want space for students to gather, talk, swap, and browse. We find it helpful to design the classroom library with sections to support this type of activity.

When we design classroom libraries, we think about how we can support students in finding books they love and can meaningfully read. When we do this work with our particular readers in mind, and when we are set up to flexibly meet their changing needs and preferences, the classroom library truly becomes the home of an active reading community. We consider

- the location within the classroom
- traffic patterns in the classroom
- space for adding or rotating books throughout the year
- sections to support instructional model.

• Location, Location, Location •

The size and shape of your classroom will clearly have a big influence on where you put your library. The library should be a central presence, but we also want this space to have a cozy, enclosed feeling. Some teachers like the classroom library to be right in the center, surrounding the meeting area. We love the message this sends when you walk into a classroom: this community is all about reading! We also understand that roaming, distracted hands may be overwhelmed by having baskets of books surrounding them during whole-class lessons. The age of your students may affect the space you choose for your classroom library.

We also consider the walls. A corner of the classroom may not be central, but it does provide two walls to enclose the space. It gives the space a cozy feeling and some privacy for conferences, partnership reading, or book club meetings. The walls also provide support for bookshelves and other shelving to display books. Some classroom libraries are spread around the room with different types of baskets of books in different areas. We have even seen a few libraries housed in converted cubby areas or closets.

• Traffic Patterns •

We often step back and observe students during transitions to see which space will be easy to access but not interrupt the traffic flow of the room. Students often meet with teachers to choose books in the classroom library, and it may be distracting or disrupting to other readers if the library is in the middle of the classroom. When we choose the location of the classroom library we think about how it impacts the work spaces around it.

• Room to Add •

We also think about how we can rotate our inventory. We always want to have enough books to support choice but not so many that we overwhelm. If the space is jam-packed, we will not be able to add books throughout the year. As our readers grow and change, we will want to add books to support their interests and instructional goals. We also want to think about how we can add books that relate to shifting units of study.

• Sections to Support Instructional Model •

Having the right book at the right moment makes all the difference in our teaching. We design the library to support the different types of reading experiences and instructional groups that take place. We typically include sections for mentor texts, small-group and partnership reading, content area reading, and independent reading. Let's take a closer look at the mentor classroom library to explore these sections (see Figure 3.6).

Author, Genre, and Content Area Reading

We organize baskets so students can find books written by their favorites authors and delve into a genre study of interest. Other students want to continue to explore the topics we are studying in our content areas. We want to highlight these books so students know where to find them.

Read-Aloud

Students like to reread, discuss, story-play or respond to texts the teacher reads aloud. We organize the read-aloud books by the month we read them so students know just where to find the book they are looking for. (See Figure 3.6a.)

Topic and Interest

This section of our classroom library is the biggest since it needs to support our students' preferences, interests, and instructional needs. Balancing the needs for scaffolding text complexity without sacrificing reader identity (as discussed in Chapter 2) is no simple task (see page 34). Keeping this balance in mind when designing the space is critical. We need to think about the flexibility of the design—is it easy to move and revise inventory? We need to reflect on the books the design is "selling"—which books are front and center? We need to make sure our inventory matches our students' interests and needs—can students access the majority of the texts in the library right now? We need to consider the attention and focus of our readers—are there too many books in the classroom library? We also need to pay attention to who owns the library—are we doing most of the library organization, or are students getting involved too?

The baskets are organized by topic, interest, and genre. There are often multiple baskets with the same label. Each basket is organized with a different band of text complexity for levels A–I. This allows students to choose books that interest them while still giving teachers a way to point readers in the right direction in terms of text complexity. (See Figure 3.6b.)

Series

Readers love to stay with a character, or group of characters, over many books. We dedicate a section of the classroom library to series. This invites our readers to see all of the options side by side to find a series of interest. We want to make sure there are options in the section for all the readers in our classroom. Teachers are aware of the level of each series so they can match books to readers while providing choice. The levels are often indicated somewhere on the book, but they are not prominent on the basket label. (See Figure 3.6c.)

Small-Group and Partnership Reading

Students love to read together and talk with each other about books. We want our students to know which books we have multiple copies of so they can plan their partner and book club reading.

Mentor Texts

We organize the mentor texts we want available to students for each unit of study in one section of the library. Once these baskets are in the library, students can access them when they are reading and writing independently. When we have a section of the classroom library set aside for these texts, not only do our students know where to go to find them, but we are also implicitly encouraging them to fold the practice of learning from other authors into their own work. Over the course of the year, we add student and teacher writing to these baskets as well. (See Figure 3.6d.)

Figure 3.6
Annotated Mentor Classroom Library

AUTHOR, GENRE, AND CONTENT AREA SECTION

READ-ALOUD SECTION

TOPIC AND INTEREST SECTION

Figure 3.6a: We organize the books we read aloud by month. This helps us find books we may want to reread or reference again. It also invites students to explore these books independently or with a partner.

Figure 3.6b: The LOL basket on the top shelf has book levels A/B while the LOL basket below has book levels C/D.

SERIES SECTION

BOOK CLUB PARTNER READ SECTION

MENTOR TEXT SECTION

Figure 3.6c: We rotate series baskets as readers develop throughout the year. We only put out series that are high interest and accessible to our students.

Figure 3.6d: These baskets match the grade's units of study. Teachers and students can find mentor texts for Author's Craft, Traditional Tales, Small Moments, and How-To.

Independent Reading
Baskets: *Then and Now*

The baskets in Figures 3.7 and 3.8 contain the same books. We took these books, which are within a band of text complexity, C–D, and reorganized them by topic, interest, or genre. The books are still leveled, but the level is written only on the book; the basket label is not a level. We have found this small change has made a huge difference for our readers. In his book *The Tipping Point*, Malcolm Gladwell (2000) taught us about "stickiness." Stickiness refers to the ability of certain ideas to become lodged in the cultural consciousness. We believe this is the case with levels in our elementary classrooms. When the most prominent basket label students see throughout kindergarten and first grade is a level, it makes sense that children will begin to identify themselves as readers of a particular level rather than readers with a wide range of interests. Since text levels are not a primary consideration of text choice throughout the lifetime of a proficient reader, we now put the level somewhere on the book and label the baskets by topic, interest, author, and genre. This makes level secondary in terms of visibility and less "sticky."

Figure 3.7: Reading baskets organized by level

Figure 3.8: Reading baskets by genre, topic, interest, and level

• Refreshing and Revising Classroom Libraries •

Readers love new books. These additions, whether brand-new or simply new to the classroom, immediately catch readers' eyes. The bookroom is a great way to refresh and revise our classroom libraries to meet the ever-evolving needs of our students, but only if the library is designed to be flexible. In the mentor classroom library, note all of the open spaces on the shelves. This is intentional. We always leave room to add baskets from the bookroom throughout the year.

Using Bookrooms to Refresh Classroom Libraries

Bookrooms allow us to continually rotate books as our readers' interests change and their skills develop. You might even consider storing some of your own books that are not appropriate for your readers in the bookroom. This way other teachers can benefit from the books you are not using. When you begin to feel your workshop getting into a rut, you can visit the bookroom to refresh your inventory.

There are certain times of the year that work well to refresh and revise our library. Holiday breaks are a perfect time to mix things up a bit. Even when we change just a few baskets, our readers take notice and can't wait to dig in! Common assessment windows are also a good opportunity to refresh. As we get to know our readers through assessment, we can change our books to excite and engage them and to fit their evolving instructional needs. We also switch out books between units of study. We might keep some books from the unit of study we are ending so students can reread and explore on their own, but we certainly swap some baskets for books that will support the upcoming unit of study. When the books change, our readers know we are about to embark on a new journey together.

We are also always on the lookout for those "hot off the press" titles. We follow blogs to find out when our favorite authors or series are coming out with a new book. Checking in with the school library (and librarian!) is another way to stay up-to-date with the latest titles. When the bookroom is stocked with new titles that will appeal to our students, we borrow them and add them to a "What's #Trending" basket in our classroom library. We suggest that bookrooms keep a section for recently published books so teachers can keep track of what is new.

Refreshing Classroom Libraries Without Bookroom Support

If you don't have a school bookroom, you can still design your classroom library so it is easy to refresh and revise throughout the year. You can look through your own books and decide which to store for future use. If you store some series, author, genre, or topic baskets, you can purposefully add them throughout the year to match your curriculum and your students' needs and interests. (See Figure 3.9.)

Figure 3.9: These extra baskets have been stored away for future use.

Some teachers work together to create their own bookroom. They combine resources and create baskets to swap throughout the year. Some even stagger the times when they teach certain units so they can share resources.

There is so much to consider when thinking about the space and design of a classroom library. We wish we could tell you there is one right way, but teaching is never that easy. Our best advice is to observe how the students interact with the space and to not be afraid to adjust it to match your students each year. We suggest you even let them get involved in the process.

Studying Bookroom Design

Just as we study mentor classroom libraries, we study mentor bookrooms before we begin designing the layout of the space. What are the possibilities? Where do schools put bookrooms? How do other schools design their bookroom spaces? Do we need shelves and baskets? Do we need cabinets or carts? How can we make the best use of our space so the bookroom is central, accessible, and functional? Let's take a tour of some different bookrooms to study the craft of bookroom design. (See Figures 3.10–3.13.)

We know that part of the joy of a DIY project is going to come from our own efforts. And while many times the hallmark of a DIY project is its imperfections, these flaws often become marks of character, points of pride, and evidence of learning.

–Kate Roberts and Maggie Beattie Roberts, *DIY Literacy* (2016, 9)

A Guided Tour of
Different Bookroom Designs

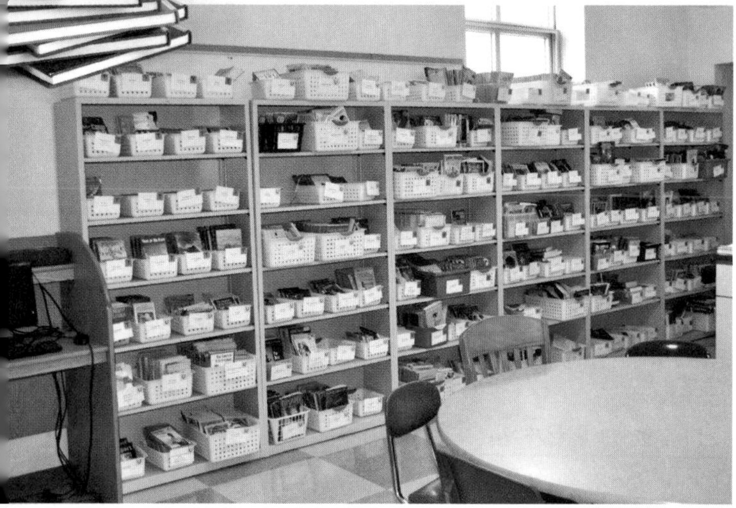

Figures 3.10a, 3.10b, 3.10c: This school is large and the classrooms are spread out across the building. In order to make it easier for teachers to quickly grab what they need, this school designed three bookrooms. One bookroom is near the K–2 classrooms, another is near the third- and fourth-grade classrooms, and the third is located in the hallway for fifth- and sixth-grade students.

Figure 3.11: This school uses a section of the school library to house the bookroom. It has series, author, and genre baskets.

Figure 3.12: This school placed the bookroom in an empty classroom. There is a lot of room for teachers to meet, browse, and plan.

Figure 3.13: This bookroom is housed in the back of the library. The shelving is low and double-sided, making it easy for teachers to browse without interrupting what is happening in the library.

Mentor Bookroom: Come on In!

We will use one bookroom as a mentor throughout this book to explain the details and specifics of each section. There are many ways to design a bookroom, and there is no one right design, location, or layout, as you saw on the tour. We chose this bookroom as the mentor because the design makes it easy for us to zoom in and get a closer look at each section (see Figure 3.14). We hope studying one bookroom will broaden your perspective and inspire you to create a design to match your needs. See Figure 3.15 for an annotated graphic of our mentor bookroom, which will show you how all of the parts make a whole.

Figure 3.14: Welcome to our mentor bookroom! This school worked together to find shelves, carts, and baskets. It was a community effort to bring this bookroom to life.

Designing Bookrooms for Access

Before you begin organizing your books to maximize access, we suggest you think about the design of your bookroom or shared space. We consider

- the location within the school
- space for adding books throughout the years
- sections that support literacy strategies, studies, and dispositions.

• Location, Location, Location •

Realtors say, "Location is everything!" and with bookrooms we couldn't agree more. Following are some things we consider when we choose a location.

Central to Everything

We look for a space that is centrally located. It helps when this is an area that teachers pass by regularly so they can pop in when they have a minute. If the space is out of the way, this will deter teachers from going by often. Also, books are heavy, so we don't want to have to travel too far with them. In some schools, like the one featured in Figures 3.10a, 3.10b, and 3.10c, we chose multiple locations. Teachers can visit any location, but we placed the grade-level texts near the corresponding classrooms.

Open to Traffic

The space should be open to traffic all day long! We see some bookrooms that are not used effectively because they are located in a reading specialist's classroom, a literacy coach's office, or a conference room. While these spaces may seem like the perfect fit for books, they are often also used to teach small groups, host teacher study groups, or hold meetings. These activities may prevent teachers from coming in and getting what they need because they do not want to interrupt the group. Teachers do not have a lot of time for planning and have to use every available minute productively. The bookroom should be a space that is open all day for people to stop in, browse, and plan.

• Room for Growth •

The bookroom will grow throughout the years, so you want to find a space that has extra room. As you design it, think about future sections or areas you might add as well as extra space in the sections you are starting with. When we are choosing a location, we like to find a space that will hold two sets of shelves that will be empty to start with; then we know we won't run out of space. We also love to envision a space for a table with some chairs. It is nice to have a place for teachers to sit and look through the books before they borrow them.

• Sections that Support Literacy Strategies, • Studies, and Dispositions

Once we determine where our bookroom will be, we create sections to support whole-class, small-group, and independent reading. Following are some examples of how we design these sections. (See Figure 3.15.)

Whole-Class Instruction

The whole-class section of the bookroom stores books that teachers use for read-aloud, to model a strategy, to study author's craft, or to support a grade-level unit of study. Teachers may borrow single titles or an entire basket of books. For example, a teacher may borrow a basket of Jacqueline Woodson books or just one of her books, like *The Other Side*, to study the use of symbolism. Some bookrooms have sections designated for each grade level in addition to a general section. (See Figure 3.15b.)

> **Interactive Read-Aloud:** The baskets of books for interactive read-aloud are often organized by grade level and include picture books and chapter books that we can peruse to find powerful read-alouds for the classroom. Interactive read-aloud baskets contain newly purchased books, whole-class sets, and old favorites. (See Figure 3.15i.)

> **Comprehension Strategies, Literacy Elements, and Devices:** We also have baskets for books teachers use to teach comprehension strategies, literacy elements, and devices. Teachers use these books to model how readers decode and comprehend as they read. While any book can be used to model a thinking

strategy, teachers often prefer certain titles for particular strategies, so we organize these into baskets for easy access. (See Figure 3.15b.)

Writing Craft: Texts are used to model craft moves a writer makes to add layers of meaning and voice to a text. These books offer relevant examples of professional writers' craft techniques or other literary devices. Sometimes these baskets are organized by genre (e.g., informational writing and fiction writing) or by literary device (e.g., flashbacks, dialogue, and structure).

Small-Group Instruction

Another section of the bookroom is dedicated to the reading students do in small groups or partnerships. There are times when we want to guide our students through the same text to model a particular strategy or introduce them to a new text structure so we think about text complexity, structure, and genre when we organize these texts (see Chapter 2, p.15). Since students often read these books with some teacher support, we indicate band of text complexity and genre when we organize them so we can easily find what we need to coach our students as they read more complex text.

Students love reading books together, so we organize many of our books with book clubs in mind. There are multiple copies of these books organized by genre, series, and author. The band of text complexity is indicated on the shelf to guide teachers in matching books to readers. Partner reading is also popular in many classrooms, so we organize pairs of books for this section. Again, these are organized to support reader choice, but text complexity is indicated on the shelf or basket to support teachers in finding books to match instructional goals and readers' developmental stage.

Independent Practice

Often the largest section of the bookroom is for independent reading. We want books to fly off the shelves, so we organize them in baskets that can easily be added to a classroom library. When teachers want to refresh their libraries, they simply browse and grab what they need. They can get several baskets at a time and add them directly to their own classroom libraries. We organize these baskets with both student interest and text complexity in mind so it is easy for

teachers and students to choose. Typically the baskets are labeled by interest, topic, author, or genre, and the level may be indicated on the inside or back cover of the book. (See Figure 3.15g.)

For the early emergent and emergent levels, we organize the texts for independent reading by mixing a variety of titles into baskets so each basket has approximately twenty to thirty different titles within a particular band of text complexity. Since these texts are short, it's important to include lots of titles in each basket to give students plenty of options when choosing independently. When we design this section of the bookroom, we intentionally create baskets that cluster some levels together into bands, for example, A–B, C–D, E, F–G, H–I. This way, students have some support when choosing texts but also have a range of texts to explore. As you can see in Figure 3.15f, all of the books on the top two shelves are levels A–B and the lower shelf has levels C–D in the baskets. The level is indicated on the shelves and on the books, but the baskets are labeled with topics such as Things That Go, Cats and Dogs, and Surprise Endings, to support readers in choosing books and developing reading identities.

Readers love to "stream" a series. We dedicate a large section of our bookrooms to different series. There is a range of text complexity represented in this section so teachers can provide choice for students. In the figures, you'll see some early emergent and emergent texts organized by series as well—so many are now available, and young readers love them! The levels are marked for the teachers, but the baskets are labeled only with the series names. (See Figure 3.15h.)

• ELA and Content Curriculum Standards •

We need books to support our grade-level standards. We find it helpful to design the bookroom with a section to support the curriculum we need to teach in each grade level. When we design this section we think about having spaces for texts that will be used for whole-class lessons, small-group lessons, and independent reading. When we want to introduce students to particular literary elements and devices (e.g., symbolism, foreshadowing, flashbacks, characters), content area topics, or authors, it is helpful to have baskets of texts that focus on those elements, devices, or topics readily available for each grade level. Teachers can easily browse and choose authors or genres for their students to study. Having the right book at the right time is often the most important instructional move we can make to support our students. When students have an opportunity to experience and study multiple texts that focus on the same literary element or topic, they construct a deeper understanding of the concept.

ELA curriculum standards focus on author and genre studies, so these books are organized to support this instruction. These are the texts all teachers in the grade level will use so students have some common experience with text throughout the grade levels. Teachers can supplement these titles with other options from the whole-class, small-group, and independent reading sections of the bookroom. Standards tell us what we need to teach, but teachers should have the opportunity to choose most of the books they want to use in their classroom. Some informational texts therefore are organized by topic so teachers can allow students to engage in inquiry projects. (See Figures 3.15c–e.)

There is also a section that houses all the informational texts needed to support curriculum standards. These are organized to support a grade level's social studies and science standards. Each grade level has a shelf with titles organized to support its content area standards. There are books for whole-class, small-group, and independent reading in these baskets. Some baskets may be empty because teachers are still selecting texts to support the content area standards. (See Figure 3.15a.)

Figure 3.15
Annotated Bookroom

ELA AND CONTENT CURRICULUM STANDARDS

WHOLE CLASS INSTRUCTION SECTION

GRADES THREE AND FOUR

Figure 3.15b: Baskets to support ELA instruction: Graphic Novels, Wordless Books, Nonfiction Text Structures, Award Winners, Fantasy, Humor, Point of View, Surprise Endings, and Leads.

Figure 3.15a: The left section houses biographies. Baskets are organized by topic (Explorers, Inventors, Influential Women) and series (Real Bios and Who Was?). The middle section houses a social studies and science basket for each grade level to support its curriculum. The right section houses a variety of topics for interest reading (Extreme Sports, Predators, Space, Animal Workers, Civil War, Cool Facts, Volcanoes).

GRADE FIVE

GRADE SIX

GRADES KINDERGARTEN THROUGH SECOND

Figure 3.15d: Baskets exploring grade level units: Homelessness, Family, and Accepting Differences

Figure 3.15e: Baskets exploring grade level units: Lists and Labels, Rhymes and Song, Perseverance, All-About, Nonfiction Text Features, Joy Cowley, David Shannon

Figure 3.15c: Baskets to support grade level units of study: Persuasive Writing, Adapted Fairy Tales, Fables, Poetry, Patricia Polacco, Kate DiCamillo

Figure 3.15 *continued*
Annotated Bookroom

INDEPENDENT READING SECTION

SMALL GROUP SECTION

INDEPENDENT READING SECTION

Figure 3.15f: This is the early and emergent reader section. To support these readers, we organize by level as well as interest (Cats and Dogs, Things that Go), series (Tiny Treasures), and topic (Science and Weather).

Figure 3.15g: These books are not organized by level although the level is typically marked inside the cover. They are organized by author and genre. Some include Kwame Alexander, Eve Bunting, and Phyllis Reynolds Naylor.

SERIES SECTION

INTERACTIVE READ-ALOUD SECTION

Figure 3.15h: Series naturally scaffold readers since there are many books at a similar level of complexity. We group the series by level of difficulty, by genre, and by topic. For example, all the adventure series of a similar level are together and all the series based on television shows are grouped together. This makes it easy for teachers to find series that will both interest and scaffold their readers.

Figure 3.15i: Some books are organized to support the work we are doing as readers and writers; some by author, topic, or genre; some by preference (funny or scary); as well as new titles.

Bringing the Designs to Life

It is not enough to make a plan. We need to set up the space and provision it so we can inventory, relocate, and reorganize the books. Following are things we often need to create a classroom library or bookroom (see Chapter 4 for specifics about how these tools are used).

• Shelving •

Bookrooms aren't always an actual room. Sometimes bookrooms are closets, movable shelves in hallways, or corners of the staff room or school library. No matter where the bookroom is located, you will need enough shelving to hold all of the baskets of books. Housing books in baskets makes it easy for teachers to grab the baskets they need and quickly integrate them into classroom libraries. While baskets maximize access, they do take up quite a bit of space. When deciding on the amount of shelving to purchase, we heed the advice of Clare's mother-in-law, Mary, "Measure twice and cut once." Think about how many book baskets will be in the room and the height of the books in the baskets. Lay the baskets out, measure, and then calculate the amount of shelving needed. Next, measure the height of a few picture books and make sure the shelving is tall enough to accommodate these books. It is also a good idea to order extra shelving so you can add new baskets of books in future years. We promise that planning this out will save hours of time.

Buyer Beware

Baskets will get a lot of wear and tear so we also think about the quality of the baskets we are using. This is not an area to skimp! We use sturdy baskets that are not too big. If they are too big they become too heavy and awkward to move around. We also don't want them too small for the size of the books— then they tip! As you are designing your spaces think about the sizing of your books, baskets and shelving!

• Book Baskets and Magazine Bins •

How hard is it to find plastic baskets, you wonder? Well, we have found that this is no simple matter—especially when shopping on a budget. Lack of planning could call for emergency measures! One school was so desperate to find baskets that the principal's mother drove to every dollar store in Massachusetts to find them. It is best to plan ahead. Here are a few tips:

- Buy baskets that are durable and can hold twenty books. Remember, these baskets go back and forth between classrooms and the bookroom and some need to hold large picture books.

- Purchase two or three times the number of baskets you need. It is helpful to have extra baskets on hand for teachers to use in their classroom libraries.

- Cardboard magazine bins sometimes do the trick if your shelving comes in different heights and you need to make the bin shorter to fit. These work in bookrooms and classroom libraries. (See Figure 3.16.)

Figure: 3.16: These cardboard bins saved the day!

Also, remember to measure your shelving before purchasing baskets. This will help you to determine how many baskets will fit on each shelf. See OR 3.1, in our online resources, for a list of where to find book baskets and bins. To access our online resources, scan this QR code or visit http://hein.pub/ItsAllAbout TheBooks-login and enter keycode BOOKS2018.

• Colored Dot Stickers •

Colored dot stickers are used to label the books and baskets so that it is easy to return books to the right place. We make a plan for how to label the books and let teachers know right away so they know how to borrow and return books. (See Figures 3.17 and 3.18.) Some teachers like to use the same labeling system from the bookroom for their classroom library. It is not at all necessary, but sometimes organizing is contagious.

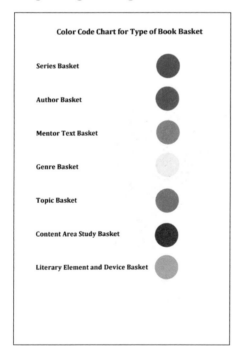

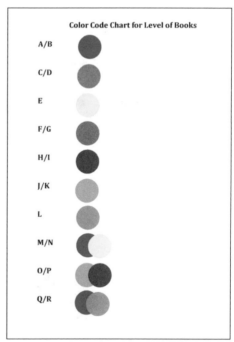

Figure: 3.17: In this school, colored dot stickers indicate the type of books in the basket. The colored dot is placed on the front of the basket and on each book in the basket. This system makes it easy to put the books in their proper places.

Figure 3.18: This school uses colored dot stickers to indicate text level. These stickers are placed on the inside cover or back of the book to help readers know the approximate difficulty of the text.

• Incidentals •

Here are just a few more necessary items to get everything up and running:

- clothespins or whatever materials you need for signing out books (see page 75 for more information on signing out books)

- pocket charts, for holding the cards for signing out book baskets

- clear book tape, index cards, or mailing labels, for creating labels for the front of the baskets and attaching inventory lists inside baskets (some schools use bin label holders like those available from Really Good Stuff at www.reallygoodstuff.com /universal-basket-and-bin-label-holders/p/159551).

Planning ahead and ordering these items make setting up the bookroom much easier. The easier the process, the quicker the books get into the hands of readers.

Story of a School: Working Together to Provide More Text Choice

The Hardwick Elementary School community spent an entire year learning about balanced literacy. Teachers, administrators, and parents were so excited to implement this model. About two weeks into the school year, though, everything fell apart. Teachers simply did not have enough books to allow students to read for thirty to forty-five minutes per day. They were already out of books!

They believed too deeply in the model to give up. Teachers organized and decided to share books. The principal found a space and organized parents to help gather, sort, and arrange books so teachers could easily share with each other. The principal gave up the conference room to house the books. It was a whole-school effort.

Each teacher selected some books to donate to the shared space. Students, parents, and teachers hauled the books to the conference room. Piles and piles of books covered the floor. These books were organized into baskets based on level, author, topic, theme, series, and genre. A simple sign-out system was designed and the room was open for business the next week.

Teachers borrowed two to four baskets each week to add to their classroom libraries. Each basket had fifteen to twenty titles in it so students were provided with a fresh inventory of books each week. Administrators planned the next year's budget to include purchasing new books for the bookroom. In the meantime, this school found a creative solution to keep students reading.

4

What Books Do You Have?
What Books Do You Need?

The Inventory Process

*Diversity is about all of us, and about us having to figure
out how to walk through this world together.*

—JACQUELINE WOODSON

Story of a Reader: If You Build It, They Will Come

Samantha runs into class on Tuesday morning and exclaims, "I was up late last night because I couldn't stop reading. I had to finish *Marty McGuire Digs Worms!* I just love that Marty McGuire."

Before Aidan, her teacher, can comment, Samantha begins rummaging through the baskets in the classroom library, searching for the next book in the Marty McGuire series. First she checks the Kate Messner author basket. Then she looks through the baskets of series books. Samantha says to herself, "I know there is another Marty McGuire book. Where is it?"

Finally, she approaches Aidan with a panicked look on her face. "I can't find the next Marty McGuire book. It isn't in the classroom library. I really need to read that book. Can you check the bookroom? Maybe it's in there."

Readers make plans for their reading. Readers know authors, series, and genres. We love that Samantha knows there is a place in her school that will have the book she wants and that she plans to get her hands on it.

Putting Time and Money Where the Research Is: Filling Our Schools with Books

It is hard to argue with research and with the experience of watching kids engage with books of their choice. In spite of this, *every school* we have partnered with over the past fifteen years has needed books. We often work with teachers who do not have enough books to support the instructional models they want to implement. We meet new teachers with empty classroom libraries and schools with no plan for how to fill them. Since books are not consumable, not a program, not a supply or furnishing, they often do not seem to find a place in the budget. We make sure that a new teacher has enough desks and chairs for his students, but we sometimes seem to assume he will arrive on the scene with his own classroom library. You won't be surprised to read that we advocate for putting our time and money where the research is—and working together to do so! This chapter will help teachers and administrators alike work together to take stock of what books you already have and what books you need.

Taking Inventory

Although the long-term goal is a rich and vibrant classroom library for every student, every year, we don't get there solely by buying books for individual classroom libraries. The first step is to *inventory* all the school-owned books (with the exception of those housed in the school library, as those serve a different purpose). This means taking stock of all the school-owned books in classrooms, storage rooms, carts, closets, and shared book spaces. The inventory process includes *only* the school-owned books, so in addition to school-owned books kept in public spaces, you do need to record any school-owned books that are housed in classrooms. Typically, this isn't many books, because so many teachers supply their own classroom libraries. We find that the types of school-owned books in classrooms are usually class sets of books or six-packs of books for small-group instruction. Some schools do purchase classroom libraries; if you are in this situation, you will want to inventory those books as well, as you may decide that some of them would be put to better use in the bookroom as shared resources.

The bookroom is a community resource, so it's best when many community members (teachers, staff, administrators, and students) are involved in the inventory process. Does this seem daunting? Don't worry! We will show you how to work together to make the process efficient and effective. Although it may feel simpler to have one or two people inventory, the results mean more when as many members of the community as possible participate. Coordinating this process takes some planning, but we think it is well worth the effort. The more people involved, the more the bookroom will be viewed as an annex to every classroom library. We suggest doing this work either at the end of one year in preparation for the next; before the students come back from summer vacation; during a school break; or during professional development days.

In most schools, the inventory process feels a bit like a treasure hunt. We find books housed in out-of-the-way places, boxed on a shelf, or still in the publisher's display and not easily accessible. Sometimes we find books in one classroom that are more appropriate for another grade level and sometimes we find texts that teachers haven't used in years. We are not going to sugarcoat it—the inventory process is a bit messy and often dusty.

If you have a space (like the future bookroom) to use for the inventory process, it is ideal to use it to gather and sort the books into piles. (See Figure 4.1.) We recommend that you and your colleagues bring all of the school-owned books to this central location. This way you can put them in piles to inventory rather than walk around from place to place with your inventory forms. If you don't have a space like this, then using the forms to record books where they are stored works just fine.

Figure 4.1: It's more organized than it looks!

Before we get started, it's important to know that the inventory process isn't meant to be exact—we don't suggest you spend hours counting books! The process and the recording forms we describe are meant to support you as you locate books and get a general sense of what's needed.

When we sort the books, we follow these steps:

1. Inventory books used for *independent reading*.

2. Inventory books to be kept in six-packs for *small-group guided practice* and *book clubs*.

3. Inventory books to be used for *whole-class lessons*.

4. Inventory books to be used for *grade-level units of study*.

5. Inventory *magazines, newspapers, and digital resources*.

Particularly if you don't have a space to physically gather and stack the books, use the inventory recording forms we've provided to keep track of what you have and to decide how you are going to reorganize the books (shown later in this chapter and provided in OR 4.1–4.8). Some like the clarity of the forms even if sorting space is available.

We look through these five lenses when we inventory so that we can get a clear picture not only of what we have but also of the role each text will serve. While this process is not completely linear and plays out a bit differently in each school, we typically begin with the independent reading section of the bookroom and move on from there. We have to start somewhere, and this section needs the most books since students spend a great deal of time independently reading, and we want to make sure we have a variety of books to accommodate all students' needs and interests. You may do it differently, but we will start with independent reading books as our first step in the inventory process.

Figure 4.2: Teachers sorting books

• Step One: Books for Independent Reading •

We gather all the single titles we have in the school. These may include books from anthologies or random collections that have appeared over the years. Some teachers also choose to donate books from their personal or classroom library collections to add to the bookroom inventory. Once all of these books are collected, we begin to sort them into piles to determine what we have and what we need.

The form in Figure 4.3 (and OR 4.1) is an example of how we might sort the single titles. If you don't have space to collect books and sort them into piles, you can count the number of books you have at each level to get an idea of which text levels you have and which you need. Record the number of single titles you have on this form.

When we record the text level on the inventory form, we typically use the Fountas and Pinnell leveling system (Fountas & Pinnell Text Level Gradient™)

FORM TO INVENTORY SINGLE TITLES

Text Complexity	Number of Narrative Books	Number of Informational Books	Number of Books at This Range of Text Complexity
A–B			
C–D			
E			
F–G			
H–I			
J–K			
L			
M–N			
O–P			
Q–R			
S–T			
U–V			
W–Z			

Figure 4.3: Form to inventory single titles

Figure 4.4: Teachers starting the inventory process

since it is compatible with many assessments that schools are using and is well known to many teachers. If your school is more familiar with DRA or Lexile levels, you can use those in place of the Fountas and Pinnell leveling system. Leveling is not a perfect science—the systems themselves aren't able to consider what the actual reader brings to a text in the way that teachers are—but we do think it is helpful for teachers to have a sense of the band of complexity or grade-level correlation of the books available to them. Regardless of the system used, we do not recommend looking up every book title to level it. Instead, spend time getting to know the characteristics of each level, choose representative trade books for each band of text complexity, and use these books as models when inventorying. This will save you time and will also help you get to know the qualities of books at different levels. Figure 4.5 lists the typical text levels of students at each grade level.

The example chart in Figure 4.6 includes some trade books we use when we level texts. These are trade books we know well so they help us remember the text characteristics of each level. We know why these books are in a certain band of text complexity, so when we have books we want to level, these examples help us analyze them in relation to the relevant text characteristics. Since we organize our books in bands of text complexity, we don't worry about whether we know the exact level of each book. Knowing that the text is in the C–D or H–I or M–N band, for example, is all we need.

We recommend teachers use our chart only as a model. The process will be more meaningful if you create your own chart using trade books that you know well. Knowing the texts is key to keeping this process simple and helps everyone feel more confident when considering text complexity. Once you decide on a system for labeling the organization of the books, you can revise this chart and add your colored coding system. (See page 52 in Chapter 3 for information about color dot systems; see OR 4.3 for a blank version of this form.) If you are not familiar with the characteristics that determine the gradient of text level, see Figure 4.7 for some resources that might help you.

We never label a basket of books with a level, and we create leveled baskets only for independent reading for bands A–K of text complexity. We do limit the range of texts in a basket for these levels because we believe readers at this developmental stage need more scaffolds and the shifts between gradients of text are more dramatic. (See Chapter 3, page 34.) We don't tend to limit the range of

fountasandpinnell.com

Progress Monitoring by Instructional Text Reading Level

GRADE	MONTHS OF THE SCHOOL YEAR									
	1 SEP	2 OCT	3 NOV	4 DEC	5 JAN	6 FEB	7 MAR	8 APR	9 MAY	10 JUN
K	—	A	B	B	C	C	C	D	D	D
1	D	E	F	F	G	H	H	I	I	J
2	J	K	K	K	L	L	L	M	M	M
3	M	N	N	N	O	O	O	P	P	P
4	P	Q	Q	Q	R	R	R	S	S	S
5	S	T	T	T	U	U	U	V	V	V
6	V/W	W	W	W	X	X	X	Y	Y	Y
7–8	Y	Y	Y	Y	Y/Z	Z	Z	Z	Z	Z

- The Progress Monitoring by Instructional Text Reading Level chart is intended to provide reasonable expectations for 10 months of the school year. School districts should adjust the expectations to align with their school/district requirements and professional teacher judgment.

- Each level indicates the instructional level; that is, the level that he or she can read with instructional support (e.g., text introduction). At levels A–K, the instructional level is the highest level a student can read with 90–94% accuracy and excellent or satisfactory comprehension, or 95–100% accuracy with limited comprehension. At levels L–Z, the instructional level is the highest level a student can read with 95–97% accuracy and excellent or satisfactory comprehension, or 98–100% accuracy with limited comprehension.

- The student's independent reading level will be one or two levels lower. The independent level is one at which the student can read without teacher support.

- If the student's instructional level matches the indicated level at the particular point in time, the student can be considered to be reading on grade level. If the student's level is higher, then the student can be considered to be reading above grade level. In this case, the student may be reading independently at the level.

- If a student's instructional level is lower than that indicated at the point in time, the student will need intervention. If the student is one to three levels lower, a Tier 2 intervention is needed. If the student is three+ levels lower, a Tier 3 intervention may be needed.

- At some points in time, students may be transitioning from one level to another (for example, Y/Z in month 5 of grade 7). That means the student is reading mostly at the lower level but taking on some texts at the higher level with success. For purposes of analyzing data, consider the lower level Y as reading on grade level.

Heinemann
DEDICATED TO TEACHERS

MK-342 10/18/2017

Figure 4.5: Progress Monitoring by Instructional Text Reading Level

Fountas and Pinnell Guided Reading Levels	Comparable Trade Books	Grade-Level Correlation	Bookroom Colored Dot Coding System
		Readiness	
A	*At School*, Jillian Cutting	K	
B	*Cat on the Mat*, Brian Wildsmith	K	
C	*Copycat*, Joy Cowley	K	
D	*Danny's Picture Day*, Mia Coulton	K, 1	
E	*Mrs. Wishy-Washy*, Joy Cowley	1	
F	*Cookie's Week*, Cindy Ward	1	
G	*Buzz Said the Bee*, Wendy Lewison	1	
H	*The Teeny Tiny Woman*, Harriet Ziefert	1	
I	*Messy Bessey*, Patricia McKissack	1	
J	*Henry and Mudge: The First Book*, Cynthia Rylant	1, 2	
K	*Frog and Toad Are Friends*, Arnold Lobel	1, 2	
L	*Cam Jansen: The Mystery of the Stolen Diamonds*, David Adler	2	
M	*The Littles*, John Peterson	2	
N	*Nikki and Deja*, Karen English	2, 3	
O	*The Stories Julian Tells*, Ann Cameron	3	
P	*Sideways Stories from Wayside School*, Louis Sachar	3, 4	
Q	*James and the Giant Peach*, Roald Dahl	4	
R	*Hatchet*, Gary Paulsen	4	
S	*The Lemonade War*, Jacqueline Davies	4, 5	
T	*Bridge to Terabithia*, Katherine Paterson	5	
U	*Number the Stars*, Lois Lowry	5	
V	*Harry Potter and the Sorcerer's Stone*, J. K. Rowling	5, 6	
W	*Tuck Everlasting*, Natalie Babbit	6	
X	*Out of the Dust*, Karen Hesse	6	
Y	*The Giver*, Lois Lowry	6, 7	
Z	*The Hobbit*, J. R. R. Tolkien	8–12	

Figure 4.6: Sample text level and correlation chart

Fountas and Pinnell Leveled Books Website:* **www.fountasandpinnellleveledbooks.com**

Scholastic Book Wizard: **www.scholastic.com/teachers/bookwizard**

Level It Books:* **http://levelitbooks.com**

Please note: The items with asterisks (*) charge a fee.

Figure 4.7: Digital resources to help determine text level

texts in independent reading baskets to the same extent for our developing and independent readers, but we still like to inventory them with text complexity in mind to make sure we have the range of texts we need. When we level texts at the higher complexity levels (S–Z), we think about levels broadly because readers at this stage can choose among a wide variety of texts. Once we inventory them, we reorganize them to reflect what a reader considers when choosing books—author, genre, topic, and interest—and make the level available only to teachers as an instructional tool.

Once the inventory form is complete, it is easy to see what you need. The school highlighted in Figure 4.8 has many single titles of fiction texts at the H–Z levels. These books can be used to create genre, author, and/or topic independent reading book baskets.

When funds become available, this school would do well to purchase books for early emergent and emergent readers (levels A–G). Early emergent and emergent readers need *lots* of books for independent reading. These

Text Complexity	Number of Fictional Books	Number of Informational Books	Number of Books at this Range of Text Complexity
A/B	25	14	39
C/D	20	16	36
E	15	12	27
F/G	28	16	44
H/I	126	47	173
J/K	168	52	220
L	150	25	175
M/N	188	51	239
O/P	150	75	225
Q/R	151	83	234
S/T	178	68	246
U/V	150	85	235
W-Z	152	74	226

Figure 4.8: Sample of a school's completed single title inventory form

books are short, so students read many titles in one sitting. We can see that this school also has fewer informational texts available for independent reading. Purchasing informational texts (especially at levels A–N) will support teachers and students as they study topics of interest and topics related to science and social studies content.

A Word About Series Books

As we inventory our single titles we are always on the lookout for series. Many readers like to read series independently, so we set them aside to organize them into series baskets. When we have books organized this way in the bookroom it makes it easy for teachers to add an entire series into their classroom libraries. If you have only one or two titles of a series, however, it doesn't make sense to organize those books into series baskets, unless you plan to buy more books in that series. As a first step in this case, we might organize several series together in one genre basket: Mystery Series, Fantasy Series, or Adventure Series. We can use the inventory form (see Figure 4.9) to note any bands of text complexity that need more series and any books in a series we would like to purchase for the bookroom.

Figure 4.10 is an example of a school's completed series inventory form. When we look over this sample inventory, we notice that there are several choices of series for students who read in the K–N text complexity range, but there are limited choices for other readers. When funds become available, this school could expand its series book collection in the following ways:

- series baskets for emergent readers
- nonfiction series book baskets
- series that feature diverse characters
- series written by diverse authors.

Once we inventory our single titles, including series books, we can determine if we have enough books to support the range of readers in our school. These figures help us calculate the number of books needed for independent reading:

Each K–1 student reads approximately five to seven books per week.

Each 2–3 student reads approximately two to three books per week.

Each 4–6 student reads approximately one to two books per week.

Name of Series	Number of Books You Have in This Series	Text Complexity	Genre

Figure 4.9: Form to inventory series books

Name of Series	Number of Books You Have in this Series	Text Complexity	Genre
Fly Guy	12	F-I	Fiction
Fancy Nancy	23	L-M	Fiction
Amelia Bedelia	54	L-P	Fiction
Splat the Cat	30	I-K	Fiction
American Girl	75	Q-R	Historical Fiction
Dear America	20	R-X	Historical Fiction
Babymouse	8	Q-R	Fiction \ Graphic Novel
Squish	2	Q-R	Fiction \ Graphic Novel
Magic Tree House	125	M-N	Fantasy
Black Lagoon	12	K-N	Fiction
Frog and Toad	40	J-K	Fiction
Mercy Watson	4	J-K	Fiction
Fox and Friends	6	J-K	Fiction
Little Critter	47	G-I	Fiction
Elephant & Piggie	7	G-H	Fiction
Cam Jansen	30	L-M	Fiction
The Littles	20	M-N	Fiction
Nate the Great	32	J-K	Fiction
Clementine	8	O-P	Fiction
Babysitters Club	12	O-P	Fiction

Figure 4.10: Sample of a school's completed series inventory form

If the school year is thirty-five weeks, you can use these estimates to calculate the number of books you need. So, if there are 25 students in a first grade classroom, those students will read approximately 125 books a week (25 first graders × 5 books per week). If you multiply this number by thirty-five weeks in a school year it totals 4,375 books. Now, we can only dream of having that many titles! Since these books are shared among all of the students, we recommend that each class needs the number of books 5–7 students will read over the course of a year (5 first graders x 5 books per week x 35 weeks = 875 books). Of course these numbers are estimates but they can be helpful when you are trying to determine if you have enough books for students at each grade level.

Tips for Reorganizing Baskets for Independent Reading

Once the inventory of single titles is complete, before we move on to the next step, we begin to think about how we will reorganize them into baskets to maximize choice for our students. We know we'll be doing the actual reorganizing down the road, but here are some questions we use to guide this process that can be helpful to keep in mind:

How Should We Organize Texts for Independent Reading?

- Which texts should be reorganized to create author, genre, and content area baskets for independent reading?

- Which texts should be reorganized to create series baskets for independent reading?

- Which texts should be reorganized to create literary device and element baskets for independent reading?

- Which leveled texts for early and emergent readers should be reorganized by topic and interest to provide more choice for independent reading?

- How should we reorganize our leveled texts for our developing and independent readers so they are choosing texts based on interest?

- Should any titles be set aside for whole-class texts or grade-level studies?

• Step Two: Books for Small Groups •

Once we've gone through all of the books used for independent reading, we inventory books set aside for small-group work. Many schools already have a section of books organized in six-packs. (If your school doesn't, you may think about adding these kinds of sets to your purchase list.) To begin this step, we gather all the texts we have in multiple copies (six-packs, anthology guided reading sets, or other guided reading texts purchased over the years) and begin to think about how we can best use these texts. In Chapter 2 we discussed that we need to use the same text only for certain types of instructional small groups (see page 15). We keep those reasons in mind as we decide which texts to keep organized in multiple copies to support our instruction and which to divide up into independent reading baskets. Most schools have more small-group sets than they need and these books sit on the shelf in magazine bins, untouched. When we take the rubber bands off and break up these sets, the books become available to several classes/students at once and kids can choose to read them on their own. (See Figure 4.11.)

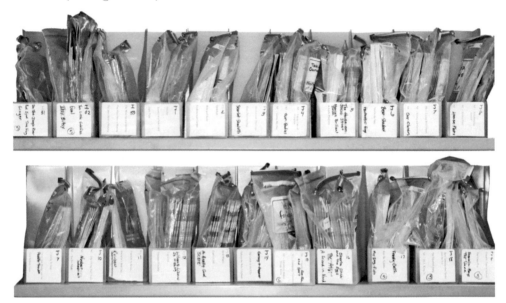

Figure 4.11: Are your leveled six-packs being used?

Again, we know we are only inventorying at this point, but here are some questions we consider as we anticipate reorganizing multiple copies of books:

How Should We Organize Our Multiple-Copy Sets?

- Which multiple-copy sets (six-packs) should we keep to support the author, genre, and content area topics we teach?
- Which sets should we keep to support book clubs and guided reading purposes?
- Which sets should be broken up for independent reading?

• Step Three: Books for •
Grade-Level Units of Study

When inventorying books to be used for grade-level curriculum—mentor texts and so on—we find that it makes sense for grade-level teams to work together. Each team considers its grade's instructional goals throughout the year alongside the developmental stages of its readers to determine what to set aside in the bookroom for curriculum studies.

When grade-level teams are taking stock of what is needed, we keep these questions in mind:

- What genres do you need at your grade level?
- Do you have books to model how readers think about elements and devices?
- Do you have books to use for whole-class lessons for your units of study?
- Are there particular collections of books by authors that you need?
- In which text levels do you need more books for small-group and independent practice?
- Do you need more books in particular content areas for your students to read?
- Do you have enough high-interest books for your students who read below grade level? Are these books diverse in terms of topic, genre, and structure?
- Do we have books that reflect the lives and cultures of our students?
- Do we have books that introduce our students to lives and cultures that are different from their own?
- Do we have books that promote diversity and equity?
- Do we have a range of book series that engage our students?

Figure 4.12 (OR 4.6) is the form we use to inventory the books we might use to support our ELA and content curriculum standards. We begin by recording the units of study we teach under the appropriate column. Then we look through the piles of books to see if we have texts to use for whole-class, small-group, and independent practice for each unit of study. These are texts we use to model strategies or mentor texts we use to study craft and structure. We record the titles we have and list what we need.

Figure 4.13 is an example of how one third-grade team used this process to determine what books they had and what types of books they needed to support their curricular content.

Once this team determined what they needed, they could take books from the independent reading and small-group sections and move them to their grade-level shelf. We need books to read aloud and books for students to read independently to support our curricular goals.

Units of Study	Whole-Class Lessons	Small-Group Work	Independent Reading
Genre/Structure • • • •			
Authors • • • •			
Literary Element/Device • • • •			
Content Area Study • • • •			

Figure 4.12: Form to inventory for ELA and content curriculum standards

Units of Study	Whole-Class Lessons	Small-Group Work	Independent Reading
Genre/Structure • Mysteries	*The Keepers of the School*, Andrew Clements *Clubhouse Mysteries*, Sharon Draper	1 six-pack of Cam Jansen mysteries, David Adler 2 six-packs of Boxcar Children mysteries, Gertrude Warner 2 six-packs of A to Z Mysteries, Ron Roy	Lots of single titles of mysteries at levels K–P. Need more mysteries at levels I–J.
• Personal Narrative	*Come On, Rain!* Karen Hesse *When the Relatives Came*, Cynthia Rylant	None needed.	Need more single titles.
• Fables	Have *Fables*, by Arnold Lobel. Need more fables to read aloud.	Need small group sets.	Need easy-to-read and new versions of fables. Are there fables written as graphic novels?
Authors • William Steig • Patricia McKissack • Bill Peet	Have individual titles to read aloud.	1 six-pack of *Sylvester and the Magic Pebble*, William Steig 3 six-packs of *Wump World*, Bill Peet Don't have any small group sets of Patricia McKissack's books.	Need authors that are easier to read.
Literary Element/Device • Character Study	*The Stories Julian Tells*, Ann Cameron *My Name Is María Isabel*, Alma Flor Ada *Amber Brown*, Paula Danziger *Judy Moody*, Megan McDonald *Gooney Bird Greene*, Lois Lowry	Have six-packs of books with strong characters: Ramona, Beverly Cleary Ivy and Bean, Annie Barrows *Freckle Juice*, Judy Blume *The Chalk Box Kid*, Clyde Bulla	Need newer series.
Content Area Study • Pilgrims • Weather • Life Cycles • Magnets	Have lots to read aloud on all topics.	Have sets of books on weather and life cycles. Need small-group sets for magnets and Pilgrims.	Need a greater range of texts for students to read independently in all content area topics.

Figure 4.13: Sample of completed inventory for ELA and content curriculum standards form

• Step Four: Class Sets of Books •

Many schools have existing whole-class sets of novels or picture books. We may keep some of these sets intact to use for interactive read-aloud or mentor texts, but we have to consider: how many sets of thirty books do we really need? If these books are gathering dust, they may be put to better use by breaking them up for book clubs (six-packs) or independent reading baskets. In some districts we have even split these sets up and swapped between schools. Knowing how frequently a title is used as a whole-class text will help us decide how to reorganize these books to maximize access. See Figure 4.14 (OR 4.7) for the form we use to inventory our class sets of books.

Title	Number of Copies	Genre	Text Level	Is This Text Used Frequently? Yes or No

Figure 4.14: Form to inventory class sets of books

Here are some questions to keep in mind as you think about how you might reorganize whole-class sets to maximize access for students and teachers:

How Should We Organize Class Sets of Books?

- Which books should be reorganized into author, genre, and content area topic baskets?
- Which books should be reorganized into literary device or element baskets?
- Which class sets of books should we keep for interactive read-aloud?
- Which sets don't we use as often? Should they be reorganized into sets for small-group reading?
- Which books should be reorganized into grade-level mentor texts for our units of study in reading and writing?

Step Five: Magazines, Newspapers, and Digital Resources

Magazines, newspapers, and digital texts are great resources that often go unused in schools. These can be reread for different purposes, shared with other classes, and stored for future use. See Figure 4.15 (OR 4.8) for the inventory form we use for these resources.

Planning Before Reorganizing

Once the inventory is done (and we have a moment to brush the dust off), it is time to review what we have and notice what we need. Taking time to reflect on the inventory and think about how to reorganize what we have to maximize access helps save significant amounts of money. Often the types of books we are missing just need to be reorganized to support our instructional needs and readers' preferences. At times we can fill the gaps in our inventory by sharing books with colleagues; by changing the way we organize the books in our classroom libraries; or by reorganizing all the school-owned books in a bookroom so all teachers have the opportunity to borrow them to refresh their classroom libraries.

Before we start moving books around, we take some time to think about the sections in both the classroom library and bookroom designs to plan the baskets we will create. You have probably already been generating a few ideas as you sorted books! (See Figure 4.16.)

If we don't have the baskets yet, we create a label for each basket anyway. As the baskets arrive we attach the labels and place the empty baskets on the bookshelves. Now when we begin to collect the books to share in the bookroom, we know just where to put them. (See Figures 4.17a and 4.17b.)

Title	Number of Copies	Genre	Text Level	Is This Text Used Frequently? Yes or No

Figure 4.15: Form to inventory magazines, newspapers, and digital texts

Figure 4.16: Planning the sections of the classroom library

Figure 4.17a: Making the basket labels as we inventory

Figure 4.17b: Getting the space ready before the books arrive

Labeling empty book baskets may seem a bit over the top but we cannot recommend it enough. Once those books start piling in you will feel a sense of urgency to get them into the hands of readers. No one wants these books going unread for a day longer than necessary. Teachers do not have free time during the day to sort books. If we set up a system when we inventory, many people can help reorganize the books quickly.

• Creating Systems to Manage the Bookroom •

If you build it, they will come! Bookrooms can quickly turn to chaos if there is not a management system in place. Creating a system can be a bit tricky. You want it to be clear so people can follow it and simple so people will be willing to borrow the books. Following are some systems that work well for us.

1. Using a Sign-Out System

When it comes to sign-out systems, we find the simpler, the better. We are always moving so quickly in schools that if the system slows us down, we tend not to use it. See Figures 4.18 and 4.19a–c for a few ways different schools organize sign-out systems so teachers can quickly grab what they need.

Figure 4.18: In order to make signing out books a simple process, this school uses a system of sticky notes and index cards. To take out a basket, a teacher writes her name on a sticky note and places it on the corresponding book basket card. When the teacher returns the basket, she removes the sticky to let others know the basket is available.

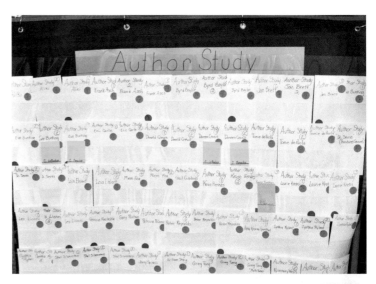

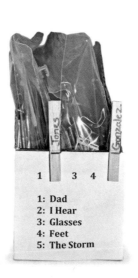

Figure 4.19a, 4.19b, 4.19c: In this system, teachers use clothespins to sign out books. Each teacher has his or her name printed on several clothespins. When a teacher wants to sign out a book basket, he places one of his clothespins on the corresponding pocket (4.19a). When he returns the basket, he puts the basket away and moves his clothespin back to the edge of the board (4.19c). Clothespins also make it easy to grab a six-pack of books for small groups. You simply place the clothespin on the title or corresponding number of the six-pack you are borrowing from the bin (4.19b).

2. Labeling Baskets and Books

When it comes to taking books out of the bookroom, we want a system to prevent bookroom books from getting confused with classroom books. This is tricky because we want the bookroom books to be integrated into classroom libraries in a seamless way, yet we want teachers and students to be able to tell the books apart. Labeling the books and book baskets clearly helps students know which books belong in the bookroom and which books stay in the classroom library. See Figures 4.20 and 4.21 for a few simple techniques to label the books and baskets to save hours of time sorting.

Figure 4.20: When we know which books will be housed in the bookroom, the first thing we do is stamp the books with the school or district name on the inside cover ("Property of . . ."). This way the books do not get confused with teachers' personal copies. Next we label the front of the book, for example BR, to indicate that the text belongs in the bookroom.

Figure 4.21: This shelf is labeled with the name of the basket so teachers and students know just where to return it.

3. Numbering the Baskets

Inevitably, there will be multiple baskets of books in each category. For example, you may have several baskets of independent reading books on the same topic at a particular band of text complexity, several baskets of the same genre, and several baskets of a popular series. In order to know which book goes in which basket, we number the baskets and the books in the basket.

Displaying essential information on the front of the book basket is key to making the checkout system easy to use for teachers and students. Look at the way the label in Figure 4.22 supports both teachers and students. These labels often show the author's name, a photo of the author, and a list of the books that are in the basket. The orange dot sticker on the label has the following codes listed on it:

- A/S indicates this is an author study basket and should be returned to the author study section of the bookroom.
- J.B. stands for the author's name—Jan Brett.
- 1 indicates that this is the first basket of Jan Brett books in the bookroom.

Each book in this basket has a matching sticker, making it easy for students to put the books back where they belong.

Figure 4.22: The label on this Jan Brett book basket provides key information for teachers and students.

Figure 4.23: The label on this author study book basket lets students know that there are digital resources available. All students need to do is scan the QR code to have more choices to read. (See Chapter 8 for more information about digital resources.)

Figure 4.24: To kick this organizational system up a notch, some schools tape a copy of the list of books in the book basket right to the bookroom shelves. This way teachers know exactly where to return the basket when they have finished using it.

If the inventory is not printed on the book basket label (as in Figure 4.22), we tape the list of books in the basket to the bottom of the basket. The list can be cross-referenced with the books in the basket to make sure we have returned all of the titles.

Rotating Book Inventory with All Calls

Your students are out of books, or they have grown as readers and your library no longer supports their needs, or your class is obsessed with mysteries and you need more, but the bookroom is empty. What do you do? Call an all call! During an all call, everyone returns all of the books he or she borrowed and the bookroom closes for a few days. The books are put back in their proper places and then the bookroom reopens.

All calls are a systematic way to rotate the inventory in the bookroom. While teachers can always return and take out new books as they need, we think it is helpful to have some formal all calls. These all calls ensure the bookroom stays organized and helps the books move between classrooms. We recommend having at least three or four all calls during the school year. These typically happen before a long weekend or a school vacation, and the dates are set by the faculty. This process helps to circulate books throughout the school and to ensure classroom libraries are refreshed.

So at this point you might be wondering who organizes the books after an all call. Different schools use different systems. Sometimes high school students doing community service projects, parent volunteers, or both, learn the system from a staff member and then complete the work. In other schools, each grade-level team is responsible for one all call a year. Organizing bookrooms can be a wonderful opportunity for family members and upper-grade students to support the school.

Story of a School: Together We Can Do So Much
Robin Pratt, Literacy Specialist, North Brookfield Elementary School

When we began working with Tammy and Clare, they told us we needed to have a bookroom. A place where teachers could go to gather baskets of books to use with their students. What a great idea! However, it was a daunting one as we are a very resource-poor district. Fortunately, we had a principal who was 100 percent on board and very talented at thinking outside the box!

We began by asking teachers to donate books—book sets, author sets, guided reading books. We had several teachers retire who very generously donated their libraries. We headed to our PTO to beg for funds. They were very supportive and committed two hundred dollars per month. OK, we were headed in the right direction. We collected Box Tops, adding one thousand dollars to our budget! Our local grocery store donated money with a point system they have set up, providing another eighteen hundred dollars to spend. Our administration added the bookroom as a line item in the budget, for five thousand dollars. We also put some titles of books we were looking for on sticky notes and placed them on the library door during a family literacy event. Parents were invited to take a sticky, purchase the book, and donate it to the bookroom in their family's name. The last place we received funds from was a Title 1 grant.

Our book baskets and bookshelves were mostly donated to the room by our staff. We begged, borrowed, and, truth be told, stole shelves from all over the building. A few even came from our homes!

Now that our bookroom is up and running, we try to keep a current Google doc with "wish-list" titles so when a few dollars appear we can get books ordered right away!

5

More Bang for Your Books
Provisioning Your School with Books

*You can't buy happiness, but you can buy books
and that's kind of the same thing.*

—ANONYMOUS

Story of a Reader: There Is More to
a Book Than the Book Itself

A group of fifth graders volunteers to give us a hand reorganizing the books in the school bookroom. They set off to create a book club section using some class book sets donated by teachers.

Ella holds a book up and asks, "What should we do if the books are ripped?"

We consider for a moment and reply, "If it is really beyond repair, we should throw it away."

The students go back to work discussing how to categorize the books.

After some time, one boy approaches. "Excuse me. Do you think this one is beyond repair?"

Clare looks up and he shows her a copy of *Holes*. It is in three sections and both covers are unattached. She responds, "I think you could call that one damaged."

"So, I should throw it away?"

"Yes, that makes sense to me."

Then, a few minutes later, we overhear him talking with a classmate. "I loved this book. I don't want to throw it away."

"Why? There are, like, twenty other copies of it. We won't miss one copy," points out his classmate.

He pauses and looks at the book. Then he heads over to us.

"Do you have any kind of tape I could use to fix this book?"

"Yes. There is book tape in that basket on the shelf." Tammy points him in the direction of a supply shelf.

We watch him carefully mend the book and place it back on the shelf. His classmate shakes her head at him in disbelief.

"I loved that book," he says. "I want someone else to read that book–the same one I read. I want another person to feel what I felt when I read that same actual book."

We are not sure he has convinced his classmate, but he had us when he asked for book tape. The next day we add his copy of *Holes* to a new basket in the bookroom, labeled Well-Loved.

When We Don't Have What We Need: Budgeting for Book Purchases

After you have reorganized the books you currently own to maximize access, it is inevitable that you will need to buy some books to expand your inventory. We realize that is not in the control of a classroom teacher to budget for a school bookroom. Administrators are the ones who have the power to advocate for making the purchase of books—authentic literature—a priority in the budget. If the mission of a district or school is to develop lifelong learners, to differentiate instruction, or to be data-driven, it needs to provide teachers with the tools to support this mission. Teachers cannot meet the needs of a range of learners without a range of books.

We need to design budgets to fund classroom libraries, school libraries, and bookrooms. While the initial purchase of books for a new classroom library or bookroom might be the most significant investment, we need to plan for the long haul. Allington states, "In planning purchases, schools need to take the long view and not attempt to stock the bookroom all at once. A five-year plan seems appropriate for bringing the bookroom up to speed but every annual budget should have some money allocated to bookroom purchasing every year forevermore (there is always wear and tear and always good new texts available.)" (2000, 86). We are often asked, "How many books do we need to buy?" We wish we had an easy answer to this question but there are many variables to consider. Book buying should be an ongoing process and a permanent line in a school district's budget. While thirty books per student may be enough in terms of quantity, the number does not ensure those thirty books are the right books qualitatively. That is why we start with bookrooms—bookrooms provide volume, range, and choice.

Every school or district we have worked with, regardless of socioeconomic background and funding, has always found the money once we highlighted the need for more books. The funding has come from different sources and the timeline hasn't always been the same, but they have always made it happen. At first, schools say they find it difficult to provide a wide selection of texts because of budget constraints. Strangely, there is often money available for workbooks, photocopying, and computers. These materials often cost the same or more than books but are typically prioritized as instructional materials. This is interesting because research has demonstrated that access to self-selected texts improves students' reading performance (Krashen 2011), whereas no evidence indicates that workbooks, photocopies, or computer tutorial programs have ever done so (Cunningham and Stanovich 1998; Campuzano et al. 2009). NCTE (2017) adds, "We strongly recommend that stakeholders do everything in their power to financially support teachers in their efforts to build classroom libraries." We realize budgets are tight everywhere and this is why a bookroom—an annex to every classroom library—makes sense. When teachers share texts and rotate inventory, stocking a school with authentic literature is a very affordable option. It truly is more bang for your books.

Don't Take Our Word for It: Thoughts on Funding from Literacy Leaders

Dr. Sheila Muir, Assistant Superintendent, Quabbin Regional School District
Initially, the bookroom was funded through our district's budget development process. The budget is guided by the district strategic plan, the district improvement plans, and our school improvement plans. Goals and action steps identified in these aligned plans are used as the basis for annual budget requests made by the principals of each school. At the time we began to plan for implementation of a balanced literacy program in our K–6 schools, we already had literacy goals in all of our district and school improvement plans because Massachusetts had recently adopted new standards for literacy. These goals set the stage for budget requests related to literacy in our K–6 schools and the initial purchase of books and items needed to design the bookroom.

Each year, we continue to set very specific annual literacy goals for our K–6 schools. The action plans that are developed to accomplish these goals include the need to continue to expand bookrooms and classroom libraries to support literacy, science, and social studies units of study that are continually evolving. The continued funding for books results from the establishment of goals and our goal-based budget development process.

Dr. Anna Nolin, Assistant Superintendent, Natick Public Schools
When we do a refresh of curriculum within a content area, we look at the texts associated with that refresh. We then budget for this curriculum refresh. I budget fifty thousand for a curriculum refresh and I do this for a two- to three-year phase depending on the scope of the curriculum changes we expect. The cost of creating bookrooms was less expensive than most initiatives. Textbooks and online resources for other subject areas is typically fifty thousand per year for three years. The bookrooms were much less expensive than that for us. For our district, it boils down to long-term strategic planning. It was helpful to start with an inventory of what we had, as we did, and then determine priorities for what we needed. We also do this for our libraries with a formal collection analysis done by Mackin Educational Resources. The inventory helped me see the scope of literacy purchases we needed so I could make yearly decisions with a long-range view. It also allows me to advocate for what we need with groups like our local education foundation, our PTOs, and any grants our development office can obtain to contribute to achieving the longer-range plan.

• Smart Shopping: Planning Ahead •

Clare's father never liked shopping with her. "You go to buy a new dress, and three pairs of shoes and a shirt later, you finally head to the dress department." He believed a successful shopping trip was focused; he shopped with his priorities in mind. While we both love a meandering shopping trip, when it comes to getting started with book shopping on a budget, we agree with Clare's father: know what you need before you begin.

The process of inventorying books reveals not only what you have but also what you need. As with the inventory and reorganizing process, we believe the work of prioritizing spending is best done as a community. So, what are some ways to make group shopping productive, efficient, and enjoyable? How we make the decision on how we will work together is often more important than the shopping method. The *group* should decide how they would like to shop together. Here are some questions to ask yourselves:

- Will we work in grade-level or vertical teams?
- Should different groups order specific text levels or different types of texts?
- Do certain groups want to focus on specific vendors?
- How can we ensure we order from a variety of vendors and publishers?
- How can we ensure that our books reflect the interests, lives and cultures of our students?
- How can we ensure that our books introduce students to lives and cultures that are different from their own?
- How can we ensure that the books in all of our book baskets promote diversity and equity?

Once we have a plan for working together and know our priorities for shopping, we need to know how much money we have to spend.

• Keeping Your Budget in Mind as You Shop •

There is nothing worse than having your heart set on buying something and then discovering you can't afford it. Before we dive headfirst into choosing books, it is helpful to figure out how much money we have and how many books our dollars can actually buy. We use the sample ordering guide in Figure 5.1 as a tool to help us stick to our budget.

Content Area Baskets (Science and Social Studies)—These baskets should be multilevel.

- 2 baskets per grade level (K, 1, 2, 3, 4, 5, 6) = 14 baskets
- 14 baskets with 20 books in each = 280 books ($5 a book)
- Approximate cost: $1,400

Author Baskets

- 6 author baskets per grade level (K, 1, 2, 3, 4, 5, 6) = 42 baskets
- 42 baskets with 10 books in each = 420 books ($10 a book)
- Approximate cost: $4,200

Genre Baskets (Including Some Nonfiction)—These baskets should be multilevel.

- 5 genre baskets per grade level (K, 1, 2, 3, 4, 5, 6) = 35 baskets
- 35 baskets with 20 books in each = 700 books ($5 a book)
- Approximate cost: $3,500

Series Book Baskets

- 6 baskets at each band of text complexity (A–D, E–G, H–I, J–K, L, M–N, O–P, Q–R, S–T) = 54 baskets
- 54 baskets with 20 books in each = 1,080 books ($5 a book)
- Approximate cost: $5,400

Literary Theme, Device, and Element Baskets

- 3 baskets per grade level (K, 1, 2, 3, 4, 5, 6) = 21 baskets
- 21 baskets with 10 books in each basket = 210 books ($10 a book)
- Approximate cost: $2,100

Small-Group Baskets (Six-Packs)

- 7 sets of books per grade level (K, 1, 2, 3, 4, 5, 6) = 49 sets
- 49 sets = 294 books ($35 a set)
- Approximate cost: $1,715

Independent Reading Baskets for Early and Emergent Readers—Baskets will contain specific levels and will be organized by topic and genre.

- 10 baskets at each band of text complexity (A–B, C–D, E, F–G, H–I) = 50 baskets
- 50 baskets with 20 books in each = 1,000 books ($5 a book)
- Approximate cost: $5,000

Total Spending: $23,315

To calculate the number of baskets needed for several text levels, multiply the number of baskets you want to purchase by the number of grade levels (e.g., 2 baskets × 7 grade levels = 14 baskets).

To calculate the number of books to purchase, multiply the number of baskets by the number of books you will put into each basket (e.g., 14 baskets × 20 books in each basket = 280 titles).

Five dollars is the approximate cost for paperback books.

Many picture books are hardcover. We estimated $10 per book and only put 10 in a basket because of the size of the books.

Early emergent and emergent readers read many books in one sitting and need lots of titles. We order these books by level and when they arrive we categorize them by interest, topic, and genre. (See page 34.)

Figure 5.1: Annotated sample ordering guide

This guide provides approximate prices per book and a system to calculate costs. All you need to do is look at the categories of books that you are interested in purchasing and fill in the number of baskets and texts you want to purchase to create your own personal shopping budget.

Buyer Beware

Books can vary in prices. The prices we list are the estimates we use. You may want to check prices in your area and shop around for hardcopy and paperback texts.

Let's look at how a few schools and teachers used the sample ordering form to create shopping lists that worked for their communities.

School A

School A hadn't purchased new books in five years. Individual teachers had added books to their own classroom libraries, but the school needed to update the collections of books in the bookroom so that all students would have access to new texts.

After completing the inventory, teachers realized that they had lots of nonfiction texts to match their social studies and science content areas but needed nonfiction texts on a variety of topics for students to read independently. They also noticed they didn't have many of the new series students were interested in reading. With these priorities in mind and a budget of $4,200, School A created this shopping list:

Budget for Ordering Books: $4,200

Series Book Baskets for Independent Reading (Fiction and Nonfiction)

- 4 baskets at each grade level (K, 1, 2, 3, 4, 5, 6) = 28 baskets
- 28 baskets with 20 books in each = 560 books ($5 per book)
- Approximate cost: $2,800

Multilevel Nonfiction Book Baskets for Independent Reading

- 2 genre baskets per grade level (K, 1, 2, 3, 4, 5, 6) = 14 baskets)
- 14 baskets with 20 books in each = 280 books ($5 a book)
- Approximate cost: $1,400

Total Cost for School A: $4,200

School B

The student population at School B was growing and in September there would be three kindergarten and three first-grade classrooms instead of two at each grade level. Before ordering new texts, School B's staff created an inventory of their books. They realized that if they used the existing titles in the bookroom, they would have enough baskets of books for author and genre studies if the kindergarten and first-grade teachers staggered when they taught specific units of study. However, with the increased number of students, they did not have enough texts to support independent reading for all of the kindergarten and first-grade students.

Knowing that they had approximately $4,000 in the budget, the school purchased independent reading book baskets for the bookroom. They wanted to help children learn to choose books based on series and topics of interest in the A–K range.

With the addition of these new baskets organized by series and topic, teachers now had more options to match books to readers and could refresh their classroom libraries with new baskets of books every few weeks. Here is School B's shopping list:

Budget for Ordering Books: $4,000

Topic Book Baskets—Baskets should be half fiction and half nonfiction.

- 4 baskets at each level range for A–B, C–D, E, and F–G
  = 16 baskets
- 3 baskets at each level range for H–I and J–K = 6 baskets
- 22 baskets with 20 books in each = 440 books ($5 per book)
- Approximate cost: $2,200

Series Book Baskets

- 3 baskets at each level range for A–B, C–D, E, and F–G
  = 12 baskets

- 3 baskets at each level range for H–I and J–K = 6 baskets

- 18 baskets with 20 books in each = 360 books ($5 per book)

- Approximate cost: $1,800

Total Cost for School B: $4,000

Teacher A

Teacher A received a $600 grant to purchase books for her classroom and she wanted to make the most of her money. After inventorying her books, she realized she needed author book baskets in her classroom library. Ideally, she would like to have multiple author baskets with individual titles for interactive read-aloud and for students to read independently, as well as multiple copies of some titles for book clubs. Like most teachers, Teacher A has students who have a wide range of interests and read at a variety of text levels, so she made sure to choose authors who write texts at a variety of levels of complexity.

Here is the ordering plan Teacher A created:

Author Baskets

- 6 author baskets with 10 books in each = 60 books ($10 a book)

- Approximate cost: $600

Grade-Level Team

A fifth-grade team did not have enough books in their individual classroom libraries to support independent reading and the school did not have a bookroom. The four classrooms at their grade level had approximately one hundred to two hundred books combined. With the help of their principal, the team received $1,000 ($250 per teacher) from the PTO to purchase books.

Instead of ordering $250 worth of books per classroom, the team decided to consolidate their money and order together. The books would be housed on a rolling cart in the hallway so that all four classrooms could access the texts. Here is how this team decided to spend their money:

Literary Theme Book Basket

- 1 literary theme book basket with 10 books = 10 books ($10 per book)
- Approximate cost: $100

Series Book Baskets

- 6 series baskets with 20 books in each = 120 books ($5 per book)
- Approximate cost: $600

Author Baskets

- 3 author baskets with 10 books in each = 30 books ($10 per book)
- Approximate cost: $300

Total Cost for Grade 5: $1,000

• Choosing and Ordering the Books •

Once we know the number and types of books we plan to purchase and our budget, the browsing begins! When it comes to getting ready to buy, we take Alexander Graham Bell's advice, "Before anything else, preparation is the key to success." Since we love to see and flip through actual books to help us choose, we prepare by gathering a variety of resources to have on hand. Here is how you can prepare:

- Call a variety of vendors and publishers and ask for multiple catalogs and free samples of some texts you plan to order. Don't forget to order catalogs of authentic children's literature, and to provide resources that give teachers access to a wide variety of text choices as well, so the group can purchase as many trade books as possible. See OR 5.1 and 7.5 for ways to find books to support an inclusive library and bookroom.

- When we speak to vendors and publishers, we explain the types of texts we want to purchase so they know what kinds of books to send. See OR 5.1 for a list of the vendors, publishers, and catalogs we use regularly.

- Bookmark the websites of vendors and publishers that the group will use and place this information on a shared drive or create a QR code. Having easy access to these websites makes ordering faster.

- Create a generic order form that can be submitted to all vendors and publishers. This form should be available in hard copy form and online for easy access. See OR 5.2 for a blank sample order form.

- Make sure there are enough laptops or tablets for everyone to use when ordering.

- Make sure all members can access the Internet on the day of ordering.

- Make copies of lists of recommended books for each teacher. See page 133, OR 5.3–5.6, and OR 7.1–7.8 for lists of tried and true books we love, organized by fiction series, nonfiction series, high-interest, easier-to-read series, and favorite authors and illustrators to study.

There are so many wonderful books, we could never list them all. These are just some we couldn't teach without. We hope you use these lists to get ideas and then create your own lists of the books you love.

Figure 5.2: Making sure we use a variety of vendors and publishers so students have access to different types of text

Figure 5.3: Discussing the books students love to determine what to purchase

Buyer Beware

In our lists of series books, we added the approximate text levels identified by the publishers. We included these levels to help you know the approximate text difficulty.
Please remember that leveling is not an exact science and a student's background knowledge and familiarity with a text structure, genre, or topic may impact complexity. Genres such as graphic novels, poetry, and illustrated fiction are also difficult to fit into the leveling system. We do provide approximate levels for some of these to give you a sense of where they might fall in relation to other series.

Book Purchasing over Time: Maintaining the Bookroom

Even if you have unlimited funding (we know—what school ever does?), we still recommend that you *do not* purchase everything at once. Order a certain portion of books, try them out, notice what books you love and what books your students love, and save a bit of money for later. As you get to know the books, you will have a better sense of what to purchase next.

You can always create the entire shopping list and then buy only some of the books the first year. This way if funds appear unexpectedly, if you need estimates for next year's budget, or if you need the financial figures for grants you are writing, you will have the numbers right at your fingertips. Following are some things to keep in mind as you refresh and restock your bookroom.

New Trends

Lifelong readers expect to have the books they want when they want them. Readers know what's up-and-coming. Readers watch book trailers, read blogs, and follow favorite authors on social media. If we want our students to be active, engaged readers we need to provide them with access to what is being talked about in the reading world. Schools set aside funds each year to keep the bookroom inventory fresh. Often we try out new titles, series, or authors in the school library. Librarians help us know what our students like and what is popular among the readers in our school. We can then order some extra copies of these in-demand titles for the bookroom.

Missing Books

What happens when books are missing? We agree with Richard Allington: "Better to lose a book to a child, than to lose a child to illiteracy" (2000, 97). Even with systems to help keep books in the correct places, mistakes do happen and a few books go astray each year. We believe this is simply part of the process and we hope these books are somewhere in the hands of a child, being read all summer or late into the evening. As books disappear, new titles must take their place. It is one reason that the bookroom needs to remain a budget line each year.

Getting Ready for the Grand Opening

G etting the bookroom up and running as soon as possible is always the priority, but we cannot forget to celebrate.

Schools are very busy places, and classroom teachers have exceptionally long to-do lists. Heading to the bookroom may not be part of the typical routine at first. A bookroom celebration can ensure everyone visits the newly provisioned bookroom early on and comes to see it as a vital resource. Once the bookroom is ready, it is critical to commemorate the moment! Following are some ideas for getting the bookroom off to a good start.

- **Ribbon-Cutting Ceremony:** Some schools have an official opening with a ribbon-cutting ceremony. Teachers and students share their hopes for this space and thank the people who were involved in bringing the vision to life. Often families and community members are invited as well so everyone understands the role of the bookroom in the school.

- **Bookroom Tours:** Tours of the bookroom are offered to teachers, staff, and administrators. These tours show everyone the final layout and organization of the books so everyone knows how to find what he or she needs. The checkout system is also reviewed during the tours so the process of how to borrow and return books is clear.

- **Faculty Meetings:** Administrators often host some faculty meetings or team meetings in the bookroom. This provides opportunities for people to browse before and after. Just being in the bookroom space invites new ideas and discussions around books. The more familiar people are with the space, the more they will use it.

Setting the Books Free! Getting New Books into the School Community

Once we open the doors for business, we cannot stop there. We need to make sure it's easy for everyone in the school community to get to know the new books. Following are a few strategies instructional leaders can use to get books out of the bookroom and into students' hands.

Bring Baskets of Books to Meetings

Before a grade-level team meeting, as coaches, we fill a rolling cart with baskets of books. For each grade level, it is important to think about the genres or authors that grade is studying and the series that students might enjoy reading. We are careful to select texts at a variety of complexity levels so teachers can find books for all of the readers in their classrooms.

After we fill the cart, we wheel it into the meeting and park it in the corner of the room. Throughout the meeting, we talk about the books, and when the meeting ends, we invite teachers to do a bit of book "shopping."

"Would anyone like texts to add to their classroom libraries?"

"I know you are studying fairy tales, so I grabbed a basket of graphic novel fairy tales. Let me know if they might work for your students."

"Here is a new series that is easy to read. I was wondering if some of your students might be interested in trying it."

When the books are right in the meeting room, it makes it easy for teachers to choose the books they need for their classroom libraries. As they find books and baskets they want to borrow, we make the sign-out system easy by recording what the teachers take right then and there.

Bring Books to Coaching Sessions

As coaches, we often hear, "I can't find a book so-and-so is interested in reading. He just flips through his books and is done in a few minutes. Do you have any he might enjoy?"

We want to anticipate teachers' needs and be responsive during our coaching sessions as much as possible. So, before we head out for a coaching session, we choose a few texts to add to our bag. Often we select a few titles that are highly engaging and easy to read. Then when a teacher talks about a student of concern, we might have a few books that she can use when working with this student. Here are just a few of the tried-and-true series we include in our bag:

Bella and Rosie, published by Pioneer Valley Books

Ballet Cat, by Bob Shea

Biscuit, by Alyssa Capucilli

Clubhouse Mysteries, by Sharon Draper

Dog Man, by Dav Pilkey

Dragon, by Dav Pilkey

Elephant and Piggie, by Mo Willems

Fly Guy, by Tedd Arnold

Fly Guy Presents, by Tedd Arnold

Hilo, by Judd Winnick

Juana and Lucas, by Juana Medina

Little Critter, by Mercer Mayer

Lunch Lady, by Jared Krosoczka

Pets to the Rescue, by Andrew Clements

Pinkey and Rex, by James Howe

The Princess in Black, by Shannon Hale

Roscoe Riley Rules, by Katherine Applegate

Shelter Pet Squad, by Cynthia Lord

Place Baskets of Books on Tables

Before professional development sessions or faculty meetings, we place a basket of picture books at each table with a sign that says, "Check out this basket of books from the bookroom/school library."

While teachers wait for the meeting to begin, they browse through the baskets. These few minutes are just enough time to spark interest in a particular title or for a teacher to learn about a new author. The books in these baskets are often conversation starters, triggering teachers to talk about the books they use in their rooms. When the meeting ends, we invite teachers to take any books that interest them.

These strategies have helped revitalize interest in the bookroom. We find the more we bring books to teachers, the more the teachers visit the bookroom. They also begin to ask us more questions about books because they see us as a resource to help them find what they need. An empty bookroom means that the books are out in the school and in students' hands. Following are several things teachers can do to help get books circulating.

Host Grade-Level Planning Meetings in the Bookroom

Grade-level teams often choose to host their meetings in the bookroom. As we analyze assessments and choose goals for students, we can select appropriate books for our readers. It is also helpful for teachers to have books right on hand as they plan upcoming units of study and focus lessons. The right book often makes all the difference in our lessons. When we plan in the bookroom, we can spend time choosing our mentor texts.

Post a Wish List for Students

Students will quickly learn that the bookroom makes their book wishes come true! If a new book is published or a hot new series is in demand, students are going to expect it to be in the bookroom. We have students post a wish list in the bookroom so we know what to order in the future. Teachers often use book-order bonus points to add these titles to the bookroom. The wish list is also visible to all, so if a family member would like to donate something to the school, the wish list is a good place to find ideas.

Host a Monthly Book Talk and Swap

Some bookrooms have a monthly all call (see page 78 in Chapter 4) to make sure books are circulating. Teachers can plan a book talk and swap as part of the all call. They take an hour before or after school to talk about some of the books they are returning—student favorites; a must-see series; an effective mentor

Offering students an engaging, diverse classroom library requires more than buying books and putting them on bookshelves. Managing a classroom library requires curation— selecting the best, most current materials for both curriculum needs and students' interest.

–Donalyn Miller, *Reading in the Wild* (2014, 80)

text; and so on. This helps teachers learn about unfamiliar books and how colleagues are using the books. When we hear someone talk about a book we often think of a student or a lesson we plan on teaching. It is a great way to build a community of readers through the bookroom.

Showcase Faculty Favorites

Some bookrooms have a shelf to display faculty favorites. It is a great visual to attract visitors to check out a new title. Teachers often include a brief description of the book and how they used it instructionally. We heard one teacher tell her class that she chose the book because Ms. Roberts recommended it. What a great way to model how readers select books!

Designate a Bookroom Day

Some schools have a day or assigned time when a class can visit the bookroom. Students help the classroom teacher return books and select new books for the upcoming weeks. When we involve students in this process, we engage them in choosing before the books even enter the classroom. They help think through which books they will take and why they are selecting those books. The more we can involve them, the more involved they will be!

Assign a Student Job

It takes some housekeeping to prepare for rotating the book-room baskets. Students need to make sure all the bookroom books are out of their book bags or bins and back in the baskets. The inventory list on the bottom of the basket needs to be cross-checked with the books in the basket. Missing titles need to be announced and searched for in the class-room. Once the baskets are ready, they can be returned to swap for new baskets. Many teachers assign this as a weekly job for students. They post "bookroom attendant" or "library curator" on the classroom job board. It is a great way to involve students in organizing and familiarizing themselves with the books in the classroom library and the bookroom.

Story of a School: Buying Books Is Professional Development

The administration at H. Olive Day School valued books. They understood that teachers need to have a voice in choosing the instructional tools they use. They also know that we are stronger when we work as a team. These beliefs were made clear when two professional development days in the district were dedicated to having teachers work in teams to select and order books.

Vendors were available with books and catalogs for teachers to browse. Each team of teachers was assigned particular vendors, levels, and types of texts. Once they researched their assignment, teachers gathered to share out and make decisions. The first session was spent browsing, reading, sharing, and comparing. Teachers left this session with lists of books by level, author, genre, topic, and series.

The next session was used for number crunching and some tough decisions. They knew what they wanted and now they had to prioritize what they could afford. They discussed the pros and cons, searched for the best deals, and convinced some vendors to waive shipping costs. One grade-level team even offered to donate some of their personal books to the bookroom to free up funds for new titles. Teams divided up to enter the purchase orders into the district database, while other teams recorded some of the instructional ideas they discussed about different texts for future use.

When the books arrived, teachers were familiar with the titles and knew the reasons these texts were ordered. It takes time to get to know all the books—especially when you are using them as instructional tools. The process of inventorying, reorganizing, and ordering the texts for the bookroom collaboratively helped these teachers get to know the bookroom texts. Such a smart use of professional development time!

So Many Books . . . How Does a Reader Choose?

Supporting Readers' Choice and Agency with Books

When there are enough books available that can act as both mirrors and windows for our children, they will see that we can celebrate both our differences and our similarities, because together they are what make us all human.

—DR. RUDINE SIMS-BISHOP

Story of a Reader: What Is a Good Reader?

Clare was meeting with ten-year-old Noah. As they looked through his reading portfolio, she noticed that each year he set the same reading goal: *I want to be a good reader.*

Wondering what he meant by "good reader," Clare decided to investigate.

"Noah, I noticed you set the same goal each year. Why did you set this goal?"

He was silent. He avoided eye contact. Eventually, Noah realized she was going to wait, and he answered, "I don't know. I just don't feel like a good reader. I never have."

Clare nodded, listening. While the diagnostic data said otherwise, Noah did not feel like a good reader. Rather than contradicting him, she decided to keep listening. Students need to be a part of the assessment process. Their goals, feedback, and reflections are essential. It is impossible to achieve change without the learner's engagement.

"I can't explain it," he continued. "I just don't think of myself as a reader. I don't feel good at it."

Clare said, "I hear what you are saying. I am wondering if your goal should match what you said: should your goal be 'I want to *feel* like a good reader'?"

He paused, looked up, and asked, "Is that a goal?"

"Yes. If that is what you want. We can talk about what readers do, say, feel, think, and wonder. We can discuss what it means to me and to you to be readers. It doesn't matter if other people tell you that you are a good reader—you need to feel it yourself."

He paused again. "Do you know how to teach that?"

Clare laughed. "I have no idea! I feel like a reader and you *want* to feel like a reader. I think together we can figure it out. Want to give it a try?"

"OK!"

This story, and so many others like it, continually remind us to focus on readers' identities. Levels, percentages, and benchmarks mean nothing if we don't also focus on developing a student's reading life. So much of our focus in reading today has shifted to measures and levels—for texts and students. The need for measurement is real, but without including the identity of the reader in the equation, we have a very incomplete picture. What makes someone feel like a reader? How do we help our students develop a reading identity? How do we honor their personal reading goals and help them choose books to meet those goals? How does our classroom library support us in developing lifelong readers?

What Is a Reader? Know Your Readers as Well as You Know Your Books

Rudine Sims Bishop wrote, "Books are sometimes windows, offering views of worlds that may be real or imagined, familiar or strange. When lighting conditions are just right, however, a window can also be a mirror. Literature transforms human experience and reflects it back to us, and in that reflection we can see our own lives and experiences as part of the larger human experience. Reading, then, becomes a means of self-affirmation, and readers often seek their mirrors in books" (1990, ix).

There is nothing more powerful than taking the time to simply talk with our students about books. When we base conversations on the interests, questions, passions, and responses of the reader, we ensure that our focus will be on the *reader* and not the *reading*. Without the complete picture—without knowing what each student is thinking, wondering, noticing, and feeling—it is difficult to connect the student to a book that will engage him. We want all of our conversations—whole-class, small-group, and independent—to begin with the readers in front of us.

Lucy Calkins and her colleagues believe that "we can't teach people if we don't know them and we can't know them if we don't listen to them" (2015, 4). How does this relate to book supply and organization, you might ask? Well, our conversations with students about their reading lives prepare us to help connect each of them with the right book at the right time. When we organize and reorganize our books into baskets that reflect the students in front of us, we let them know that they are the centers of their reading lives—and at the same time, we learn what we need to know to suggest books that will be a good fit.

We encourage students to join us in reorganizing books. Often the kids themselves will come up with a topic, study, or type of book to make a basket for, and then they help us find books in the bookroom and the classroom library to fill those baskets. (See Figure 6.1.) This not only revitalizes the classroom library but also helps students think about books in new ways.

Talking with Your Students About How Readers Choose Books

Dorothy Barnhouse highlights the importance of focusing on how readers know what they know in a text, instead of teaching the text itself. "Emphasizing *what* over *how* in our instruction means we have often failed to pay attention to what conferences reveal—namely, that students at every level need instruction to make visible the way texts work and the thinking that readers do as a result" (2014, 95). In our guided instruction, we actively find books, create new baskets, and make plans to gather texts for future studies. We set instructional goals with students and then immediately head to the classroom library

Figure 6.1: Kids love to create text sets for the library

to think about what books will best support the work of that goal. Books are the bridge between our students and our instructional goals. If we don't have the books we need in the classroom, we head to the bookroom to find what we need. (See Figure 6.2.)

In the sections that follow, you'll find ideas about what readers consider when they choose books—ideas that will support you in finding just what books your students need and in helping them do this work for themselves.

What Readers Consider When Choosing Books

- community
- interests and preferences
- projects and inquiry
- habits and dispositions
- life events
- goals.

Figure 6.2: The bookroom and the classroom library work together to support reading communities. Teachers can take entire baskets and incorporate them into their classroom library.

• Readers Consider Community: •
I Want What He's Reading!

When we reflect on our own reading lives, we realize that they are almost completely driven by community. We are both in book clubs in our neighborhoods. We contribute weekly to online communities such as "It's Monday! What Are You Reading?" (#IMWAYR), join the Twitter chat #titletalk monthly, read the *Nerdy Book Club* blog, and even join nErDcampMI to connect with other educators about children's books and professional books. We are on Goodreads and follow what friends and colleagues are reading. We subscribe to many blogs that update us on what's new in children's literature. We read what other members of our professional and personal communities are reading. (See Figure 6.3 and OR 6.1) As adults, we do not form book clubs based on our reading levels and we need to make sure this is not the only small-group experience our students have in school. They need to know that readers often consider what their peers are reading when they choose books. Engagement in text is often social—it is about being a member of a community.

So what can book access driven by the consideration of community look like in the classroom? Sometimes students will choose books based solely on recommendations from friends or siblings—or even just from seeing what loved ones are reading—without considering whether or not those books are a good fit for them as individuals. If you notice a group of kids who are in this boat, you might support their desire for reading community by setting them up in a book club together. We often invite students to think about the types of texts or topics they want to read together as a book club, and then we help them find a book that will fit that need. To do this work well, it is so important that we take time to show our students how books are organized to support their reading community.

When building a classroom library, we make sure to include multiple copies of some titles to support this type of social reading. And when the classroom library has a single copy of books students are interested in reading together, we can go to the small-group section of the bookroom to find the additional copies they need.

We've Got a Book for That!

Organizing Books to Support a Reading Community

Here are some baskets of books we created with students to support reading in a community:

Books to Enjoy with a Partner

Series to Read with a Group

Read It and Rate It—Should We Get Multiple Copies?

Topics to Explore with a Book Club

Plays to Read Together

Fiction and Nonfiction Paired Sets

Poems for Two Voices

Listen Together and Talk

Books to Read and Reread

Read-Alouds to Reread and Discuss

Let's Stream This Series

Here are the blogs, websites, Twitter chats, and podcasts we rely on to learn about new books. We love being a part of these communities.

- *Nerdy Book Club*: Each day, Nerdy Book Club features a new blog post about children's literature. These posts are written by educators, librarians, children's book authors, and readers, who all love children's books (**https://nerdybookclub.wordpress.com**).

- *Donalyn Miller's SlideShare Decks*: Each year, Donalyn Miller creates a SlideShare of her favorite books published during the year (**www.slideshare.net/Donalynm/best-books -of-2016-so-far-march-2016-by-donalyn-miller**).

- *The Yarn*: Colby Sharp and Travis Yonker interview children's book authors about their latest books at The Yarn (**http://blogs.slj.com/theyarn**).

- The *Our Story* app from We Need Diverse Books: This app lets readers, teachers, educators, and librarians search for books. This tool helps you find books with diverse content and by creators from marginalized communities. To learn more about this incredible resource, listen to Dhonielle Clayton, chief operating officer of We Need Diverse Books, explain how this app works at **www.diversebooks.org /ourstory**.

- *#titletalk*: At 8:00 p.m. EST on the last Sunday of each month, Donalyn Miller and Colby Sharp host a chat about teaching reading and children's literature (**https://twitter.com /hashtag/titletalk?lang=en**).

- *A Year of Reading*: On their blog, Franki Sibberson and Mary Lee Hahn share the new books they are reading with their students (**http://readingyear.blogspot.com**).

- *It's Monday! What Are You Reading?*: Jen Vincent and Kellee Moye host this virtual group on Mondays where educators share their blog posts about the books they are reading (**www.teachmentortexts.com**).

- *A Teaching Life*: On this blog, Tara Smith shares books, poetry and teaching ideas from her sixth grade classroom (**http://ateachinglifedotcom.wordpress.com**).

- *Nonfiction Picture Book Challenge*: Each Wednesday educators share the nonfiction picture books they are reading. This blog is hosted by Alyson Beecher (**www .kidlitfrenzy.com**).

- *Picture Book 10 for 10* (#PB10for10) and *Nonfiction Picture Book 10 for 10* (#NF10for10): This Google+ community is hosted by Cathy Mere and Mandy Robek. On February 10 educators post their top-ten nonfiction picture books and on August 10 educators post their top-ten fiction picture books (**https://plus.google.com/communities/109 747361653807401083**).

- *Watch. Connect. Read.*: On this blog, Mr. Schu shares book trailers for new books (**http:// mrschureads.blogspot.com**).

- *Read, Write, Reflect*: Katherine Sokolowski shares insights, books, and reflections from teaching seventh grade (**http://readwriteandreflect.blogspot.com**).

- *nErDcampMI*: Each July, we travel to Michigan to learn alongside fellow educators, librarians, and children's book authors. This conference is inspirational and chock-full of learning. We leave with a stack of new books to read and a list of titles that will be published in the fall (**http://nerdcampmi.weebly.com**).

Figure 6.3: Our virtual reading community

Sometimes a group of students will naturally form a book club around a common interest—for example, a group of third graders that Clare encountered wanted to learn more about the *Titanic*. Because both Clare and the classroom teacher knew that the bookroom housed books that would support their club, they were off and running. This particular school's bookroom had bins of books organized by topic that included a wide range of text complexity (including audio); one of those bins focused on the *Titanic*. Each reader in the club was able to find books that matched his or her personal reading goal, his or her academic needs, and the club's focus. This fact set up each member to contribute to the group based on his or her own reading. When readers choose by shared interest they can connect with each other both socially and academically.

• Readers Consider Interests and Preferences •

Louise Rosenblatt's transactional reading theory (1938) suggests that text becomes a text only when a reader, at a specific moment in time, brings the aggregate of his or her life and literary experiences, attitudes, and values to the work. Without the reader there is no text. "The reading of any work of literature is, of necessity, an individual and unique occurrence involving the mind and emotions of some particular reader and a particular text at a particular time under particular circumstances" (Rosenblatt 1985a, 40). This theory has been on our minds lately as we've conferred with students and thought about how to use texts to engage and teach them. The reader's schemata—what he knows and has experienced—matters.

Research also indicates that a text that is familiar to us in structure, content, or topic is easier to comprehend. "According to schema theory, context-reliant reading is effective and accurate when the reader possesses sufficient background knowledge and has a schema for the material" (Farstrup and Samuels 2002, 191). A reader's prior knowledge creates a powerful advantage that facilitates accuracy and comprehension (Recht and Leslie 1988; Rumelhart 1980; Farstrup and Samuels 2002). These studies demonstrated that when readers either chose a text that was familiar in topic, content, or structure, or chose to engage in a study of a text type over time, their engagement, accuracy, and comprehension improved.

How does this play out in the classroom in terms of book organization? See the following "Peek into the Classroom" to find out how one teacher organizes and uses baskets with readers' preferences in mind.

We've Got a Book for That!

Organizing Books to Support Interests and Preferences

Here are some baskets of books we created with students to support interests and preferences (see also Figures 6.4a–c):

Tear Jerkers

LOL!

Sports

Surprise Endings

Characters You Love to Hate

Strong Girl Characters

Series You Read in Order

It's Also a TV Show

Gross Topics

You Won't Believe It

Figure 6.4a, 6.4b, 6.4c: Examples of books organized by interests and preferences

PEEK INTO THE CLASSROOM

Tammy met with a group of third-grade readers who were having difficulty sticking with a book, to show them how readers think about interests and preferences when choosing books. She started by asking them what they noticed about themselves as readers. "So, what are you noticing about your reading? How is reading feeling for you?"

Silence. She waited, pen in hand, signaling she knew they had something important to share.

"Not great."

"Me too."

"I can't seem to get into a book."

"Exactly. I just keep switching between books and can't finish one."

Tammy paused, making sure they were finished sharing, and then responded, "I am so glad you are telling me this. Let's talk more about what is happening for you as a reader. I want to know. Can you talk to me about what is in your reading bag and why you think you keep switching or can't get into a book?"

One by one they dumped their bags, leaving a huge pile of books in the middle of the circle.

Tammy laughed. "Well, I might be beginning to understand the problem."

The students began to laugh as well and the ice broke.

"So talk to me about how you chose these books. You each have a lot of books in your bag."

"Well, I just go to the M bin and choose a bunch. I usually pick six to seven books to have in my bag," one student replied.

"I choose, like, three from the fiction M bin and three from the nonfiction M bin," another explained.

"I choose chapter books," a third added.

Tammy decided to build on what they knew and talked to them about how readers consider interests and preferences when they choose books. "Each of you is thinking about the type and number of books you are reading. Those are important considerations. But readers *also* consider their interests when they choose books. They think about what they like in life and use that to help them pick. So talk to each other about some of the books in your pile—do you like them?"

As the students talked, Tammy noticed they weren't talking about the types of books they liked (funny, scary, sad) or the types of characters they enjoyed (brave, adventurous, silly). She decided to model a bit. "When I choose books, I think about the types of characters I connect with and the kind of stories I prefer. For example, this book, *The Littles*, is one I love to read. There is always some tension in the story, but I know it will end happily. I love the personalities of the Littles—they are funny, clever, and brave. Once I find a type of book I like, it is easier to find others. Let me show how your library is organized to help you choose books to match your interests."

Tammy showed them some book baskets she borrowed from the independent reading section of the bookroom. These baskets were organized by series or type of book.

"This basket has all the Littles books in it. It is a series, so there are lots of books with these characters. I might decide to choose all my books from this basket. Readers often get hooked on a series and stick with it.

"This basket has all funny books. If I am in the mood for funny, I can choose all my books from this basket. This book, *Marvin Redpost: Class President*, is funny and it is also a series. If I like it, I might head over to this Louis Sachar basket next week to choose books. If he wrote one funny book, chances are he wrote others.

"When readers choose books, they think about what they like and their interests. Books are organized to help you choose with those considerations in mind. What do you think?"

The boys all started to talk at once.

"I like scary books. Is there a scary basket?"

"I like reading books with the same characters; then I don't have to remember all the new people in each book. There is usually only one book of a series in the M basket."

Tammy nodded. "That is important to notice. If you find one you like and it is part of a series, we can go to the bookroom and get the series basket for you."

"That would be awesome! Do you have Ivy and Bean? I love Ivy and Bean!"

Part of our work with matching books to readers is to teach our students how readers choose books based on personal interests and how the classroom library is organized to support their preferences. When readers can look at a library and see themselves in it, they are more likely to choose a book that engages them personally. Once we know what engages them and what doesn't, we can support them in finding texts that match them in terms of text complexity by the ways the books are organized in the bookroom. Even if they do not prefer a book, we want to know why. When we take the time to listen, we will understand our students better and be able to help them find books that will engage them.

• Readers Consider Projects •
and Inquiry Studies

We meet many readers who get invested in a topic and do not want to shift from reading about it. Teachers often ask us if this is a problem. Should we worry if they will read only about one topic? For our nonfiction reading, both of us choose mostly texts about teaching reading and writing; our husbands could certainly argue that there is not a range of topics on our bookshelves. Many adult readers choose to read in depth about what they want to learn. How can we help our students choose books to support their own personal inquiries? How can we show them that choosing books based on what they want to learn often leads us to new territories to explore?

PEEK INTO THE CLASSROOM

Clare was conferring with a reader who loved learning about the presidents of the United States. She was reading extensively about many of the presidents. Clare decided she wanted to know more about this student's passion.

"I would love to know why you love reading about the presidents. What do you find so interesting about them?"

"I like to read them in order. I like to know all the facts about each president. I memorize the same information for each one."

"Interesting. Have you found anything in common about them?"

The student paused to consider this and began flipping through her notes. "You know, a lot of the recent presidents get dogs. There is a lot about that and I didn't find that information about the earlier presidents. I had to add that section." She pointed to show her notes.

Clare took a closer look at her notes. "That is interesting. I wonder why. Which president was the first to have a dog?"

"I don't know. I would have to go back and check them all for dogs. One may have had a dog but I just didn't notice. I wonder when people in the United States started having dogs for pets. Did we always have dogs for pets?" the student wondered.

"Sounds like you have a few topics to research—presidents and dogs, and when dogs started to be pets. Are you planning to do that work? How will you find books?"

"I have read all the books on presidents in the classroom."

"Let's go to the independent reading section of the bookroom and see if we can find some other resources." (See Figure 6.5.)

Figure 6.5: Taking time to show a student how books are organized is time well spent.

Book choice is personal. As we confer with students and ask them why they are reading a particular book or what they are learning, it helps us think about options for them. When we look into the eyes of a student and say, "I saw this book and thought of you," we do more than match a book to a reader. We engage her as a person. When someone thinks of us, about us, we cannot help but want to engage. It means "I matter," "I am important," and "I am accepted." We find there is no better way to engage our students than to let them know we are thinking of them . . . and then hand them a book. Better yet, we can show them where we found the book and how the books are organized to help them find books that propel their inquiry and thirst for knowledge.

We've Got a Book for That!

Organizing Books to Support Projects and Inquiry Studies

Here are some baskets of books we created with students to support projects and inquiry studies:

Books About Extreme Sports

Books About Houdini

Books About Olympic Stars

Books About Americans Who Changed Our History

Books About Kids Who Make a Difference in Our World

Books About Designing Experiments

Books About Predators

Books About Learning How to Draw

Books About Horses

Fairy Tales to Compare and Contrast

• Readers Consider Habits and Dispositions •

Readers make plans. We cannot imagine packing for a trip without planning our reading and locating the local bookstore or library. We always have a book on hand in case a quiet moment presents itself. We expect to read every day. We expect to talk and respond with other readers every day. These are just some of the habits and dispositions that build a reading life. How can we help young readers to build their own reading lives? And how does book organization support them in developing the habits and dispositions of a reader?

Readers Plan for the Pace of Life

When we talk with students about their personal reading goals, we always ask about when they tend to read. It is important to know what is happening in your life and make a plan to fit what is going on or coming up. Clare thinks a lot about her reading during baseball season. She knows she'll have a lot of down-

We've Got a Book for That!

Organizing Books to Support Readers' Habits and Dispositions

Here are some baskets of books we created with students to support planning for the pace of life:

Magazines

Books You Can Finish in a Week

Books You Should Read When You Have a Long Period of Time

Series You Won't Want to Start Until You Have Time to Finish

Beach Reads

Books to Pack for Long Car Rides

Books with Ideas of Things You Can Make

Books You Don't Have to Finish in One Sitting

Books That Have Chapters Told from Different Characters' Points of View

Books You Can Read Online

time while waiting for her son to be done with practice or for a game to start. She tends to choose short texts for this time of year so she can finish a few titles a week during this season.

We also think about vacations when we plan our reading. Some vacations have more downtime and others are very social. We save some books for when we know we will have long periods of time to read. Those series you want to stream or binge-read are great to save for summer. (For suggestions about helping students plan for summer reading, see page 123.) Other books might have a more challenging text structure and you know you will need to have more focused time to engage in the story. Readers plan for the time they have and make sure the books they choose match the time they have available. Reading is an important part of life, but only if you plan for it. When we talk with readers

We've Got a Book for That!

Organizing Books for Our Mood

Here are some baskets of books we created with
students to recognize their mood:

Survival Stories

Books with Silly Characters

Books That Require a Box of Tissues

Books That Won't Let You Turn the Light Off

Page-Turners

Books About Friendships

Stories About People in Faraway Places

Poems to Make You Laugh

Cliff-Hangers

Books About Kids Solving Problems

about what is happening in their daily lives, we can help figure out ways to make reading a priority. We believe being a reader means you find time to read, and our students need to know this too.

Readers Are Moody

It is important to consider what you are in the mood to read when you choose books. Our frame of mind can impact what will or will not work for us as readers. Sometimes we need to escape or to laugh. Other times we need a good cry or scare. When we think about what release we need in our life or the feeling we want to feel, we can choose a book to help us get there. When we talk to our readers about what is going on in their lives, we hear about their worries, frustrations, and joys. We can let them know that readers choose books to help them get through or celebrate times in their lives.

Readers also need to know that sometimes we think about mood in terms of our cognitive availability. After Clare finished *The Goldfinch*, by Donna Tartt,

We've Got a Book for That!

Organizing Books for Choosy Readers

Here are some baskets of books we created with
students to support choosy readers:

If You Liked _____, You Will Love

Books That Have Won Awards

Coming Soon

Newly Released

Books We Read Aloud This Year

Other Books by the Authors We Read Aloud

Favorites from [Another Teacher's] Class

Class Recommendations

The Principal's Favorites

Longest Waitlist in Local and School Library

she needed a break. She loved it, but it was long and dense. She found herself needing to reread many parts and dip back into the text often in order to fully understand it. She wanted to find some quick, easy reads after that book. Whenever it is ski season, Tammy knows she will be spending a lot of time in ski lodges by the fire, waiting for her family to return from the slopes. This area is loud and busy—full of distractions. She likes to find books that grab you from page 1 and are easy to put down and pick up again during ski season. It is important for readers to consider what they are up for in terms of challenge, length, and familiarity when they choose a book.

Readers Are Choosy

We use social media to keep apprised of what is upcoming and what is getting great reviews. Just like moviegoers, we use trailers, previews, and reviews to guide our choices. Readers consider the opinions of other readers when they choose books. We want to make sure our students know they have a right to be picky when setting their personal reading goals. We want to show them where they can find recommendations, previews, and reviews to guide their choices. Figure 6.6 (OR 6.2) lists some of our go-to sources for these tools.

Book Trailers

At Scholastic's website for kids, students can log in and watch book trailers and interviews with authors and see book recommendations from celebrities. Go to **www.scholastic.com/kids/videos.**

Book Trailers for Readers has podcasts and trailers for books that have been nominated for the Sunshine State Young Readers Awards. Readers can see the covers of the nominated books and can click on a cover to watch and listen. Book Trailers for Readers also has book trailers made by students. Students can watch other students' book trailers and submit their own. Go to **www .booktrailersforreaders.com/Home+Student+Book+Trailers.**

Book Reviews

Three times a year, students at the Center for Teaching and Learning (Nancie Atwell's school) help their teachers create grade-level lists of books they love. Go to **http://c-t-l.org/kids-recommend** to see the grade-level lists they share on their website.

Scholastic's website has a place where students can read other students' reviews and submit their own reviews. The reviews are organized by genre and grade level to make it easy to search for books to read. Go to **http://teacher .scholastic.com/activities/swyar.**

DogoBooks is filled with book reviews. Students can read the reviews and submit their own at **www.dogobooks.com/page/2**. DogoBooks also has links to online book clubs at **www.dogobooks.com/book_clubs.**

Figure 6.6: Trailers and reviews help readers choose books.

Figure 6.7a, 6.7b: We can also make recommendations through how we organize our books. If we spend time honoring students' book choices, they will spend time finding books they love!

• Readers Consider Life Events •

Many readers are pragmatic; we read to get information about things that are important in our lives or problems we need to solve. Tammy is planning to build a brick oven in her yard, so she has been reading lots of books to help her learn how do it and what she will need. We both have read tons of parenting and gardening books throughout the years as well. Clare's family members read about all the NFL teams when they prepare for the fantasy football draft. When real things happen in our lives, we want to read about them to learn more and prepare! In our conversations and conferences with our students, we want to pay attention to what is happening in their lives. We want them to know that if they are worried about or looking forward to something, they can read about it to learn more. Reading gives us power and helps us feel prepared to encounter the victories and defeats in life.

We've Got a Book for That!

Organizing Books to Support the Events in Our Lives

Here are some baskets of books we created with students to support thinking about life events:

Travel Guides

Family Milestones

Everything You Ever Wanted to Know About Summer Camp

Books About Cities

Books About Pets

Best Places to Visit in Your State

Books About Visiting Relatives

Finding Fun Projects to Do

Books About New Siblings

Books About the Seasons

Readers Get into Ruts

There are times when life gets busy or we get into a rut and lose our reading identity. When Clare's mom passed away, she was unable to read for pleasure for eight months. Her mind wandered, she lost track of the plot, and she couldn't connect with the characters. She could read for information or for her job, but not for entertainment. Her brain would just not focus. She tried lots of different types of books and modalities—paper, digital, and audio. She tried reading at different times of the day and in different places. Her heart just wasn't in it and her brain followed suit. As an adult she had control over her reading life, which allowed her to find her way back to reading. This helped us realize how important it is to talk with our students about how reading is going for them and be open to the feedback they give us. We need to honor how they are feeling

We've Got a Book for That!

Organizing Books to Help Readers Get Out of Ruts

Here are some baskets of books we created with students to help them get out of ruts:

Books You Could Read Again and Again

Comics

Sports Magazines, Fashion Magazines, Fishing Magazines

Bored with What You Are Reading? Try This!

Books with an Interesting Format

Same Story, New Structure

Books Written by Authors in Our Classroom

Stories to Read in One Sitting

Books to Listen To

Song Books

Books to Inspire You—Look at What Kids Can Do!

Civic Action—Finding Ways to Help Others

and provide options for them to engage and connect personally with books. A reading life is a journey and we need to validate all the stages we may encounter.

• Readers Consider Goals •

Research demonstrates that you cannot meet a goal if you are not aware of the goal you are hoping to achieve (Wiggins 2012; Black and William 1998). Teachers need to know what students are hoping to achieve personally and introduce them to the types of things readers often want to achieve. When we ask our readers what they want to work on or achieve as a reader, we often hear comments like these:

"I want to read better."

"I want to decode hard words."

"I want to be a level L."

"I want to read quickly."

We've Got a Book for That!

Organizing Books to Help Support Our Goals

Here are some baskets of books we created with students to help them pursue goals:

Try a New Genre

Characters Learn Big Lessons

Settings Matter

Various Points of View

The Plot Thickens

Following the Story Through Multiple Characters

Who Said What? Following Dialogue

Flashbacks

Settings I Don't Know

Why Did He Do That? Thinking About Motivation

We want to dig a little deeper, so we ask them to tell a little more. "What do you mean? Why do you want to achieve this? Why types of books help you meet your goal?" Then we hear again and again, "I want to read long books," "I want to read hard books," or "I want to read big books."

We don't know about you, but we have never walked into a bookstore or a library and requested a big, long, hard book. It's just not what we consider as readers. We wonder if our readers know what to consider other than text difficulty, length, and rate. These seem to be the go-to answers because our students believe this is what society values. Over the years, we too have found ourselves in situations where we told a reader, "That is too hard," or, worse yet, took a book out of the hands of a reader. We try to avoid this at all costs and here's why: human nature! Neither of us responds well to someone telling us what we can't do. Who does? Reading is personal and our interactions make a difference in how a person identifies and feels about it.

We are not suggesting that we allow students to read frustration-level texts for weeks on end. We do, however, tend to look for the long win rather than the quick win. Instead of taking a book away, we ask, "Why did you choose this book? Tell me why you love it." The answer often guides us. When we listen to the *why* behind the book choice, we know how to steer the reader toward a text that will engage her personally and allow her to meaningfully interact with the text academically. The reader needs to be a part of the decision and needs to see herself in the choice. We are honest with students about text complexity. We do not shy away from talking about the difficulty of text—its length, structure, vocabulary, or themes. We just make sure that the conversation is about the book, not the reader. It is not that the reader is not good enough; it is that the text is not the right choice at this time for this purpose. We find ourselves in these conversations all the time—how often have you encountered a student who desperately wanted to read all of the Harry Potter books when those books weren't yet a great instructional fit? In cases like that one, we let the student know he is welcome to read Harry Potter (or whatever book he is attached to) outside of school, but we will help him find a similar book or series that will be a better fit for classroom work. Our knowledge of the books at our disposal and our ability to find those books when we need them ensure we'll be able to match that student with a book that will excite him just as much.

We need to listen to our readers' personal goals and help them meet those goals within the context of our instructional and curricular goals. Our students need honest and specific feedback in order to grow as readers. We too need to hear our students' honest and specific feedback. The feedback loop is critical to growth, and our conversations with students need to encourage this type of dialogue. As Jennifer Serravallo reminds us, "you could be the most eloquent teacher, the best strategy group facilitator, the most insightful conferrer. But if you send your kids back for independent reading and they don't read, then they won't make the progress you are hoping for" (2015, 44).

Goals are meaningful only if they lead our students to a book. The habits and dispositions of a reader need to be at the center of all of our students' goals. If we teach the reading rather than the reader, we have not inspired them to be life-long readers. If you are looking for a resource to help you set meaningful goals with students, goals that will make them run to the classroom library, check out *The Reading Strategies Book*, by Jennifer Serravallo (2015).

Helping Students Plan for Summer Reading

Each year we spend a week or two at the end of school helping readers make a reading plan for summer vacation. The first step we teach our students is to think about when they will have time to read. Will they be spending more time at home? Are they going away? Visiting family? Are plans still undecided? Students talk with their families to see if there are any specific summer plans. We give students a summer calendar that shows when school will end and when it begins again so that they know how many days they have to plan.

We also want our readers to think about where they will read. Will they spend more time in a car or on public transportation? Will they be away or stay at home? This information will help them devise the best plan they can.

Tips for Summer Reading

1. Read in the car or when traveling on a bus.

2. Begin each day with reading before it gets too hot.

3. Partner-read with a parent or caregiver.

4. Read books to a younger child, a friend, or a neighbor.

5. Keep books in a bag so that they are easy to grab.

6. Keep books in a spot where you can find them.

Now that our readers have some ideas about when and where they will read, we ask them to think about what they want to read. The independent and small-group reading sections of the bookroom have baskets to help students decide so they can make a plan.

Summer reading affects student achievement, and schools are working hard to find creative ways to get books into students' hands. Following are a few different ways we have helped schools make summer reading possible for all students.

• School Book Swaps for Vacations •

Each spring some schools organize a whole-school book swap. They ask families to look through their bookshelves and find children's books that they would be willing to donate to the swap. What typically happens is that some families donate many titles, whereas others donate only a few. To ensure that they have enough titles for the swap, teachers, librarians, and literacy coaches also look through school libraries, classroom libraries, and the school bookroom for titles that could be added to the swap.

Once there are enough books, a few volunteers and teachers organize the books so that students can begin selecting some for summer reading. Students in the younger grades usually select books first to ensure that they find books that match their personal and academic goals. These books are placed in summer reading book bags and sent home for the summer. One school even adds a bookmark and a book light to each bag as small gifts for the students. What if you don't receive enough donations? In one school, many students did not have books to contribute, so they reached out to a school in a different community for help.

• Summer Book Appointments •

Another way schools help readers to continue reading over the summer is through summer book swap appointments. All student appointments are scheduled on the same day of the week so that only one staff person is needed each week. The student simply meets a teacher or administrator in the bookroom, returns the books she has finished, and picks new titles to read during the upcoming week. It takes only a few minutes, but this check-in and supply of new books keeps many students reading all summer.

How do you find staff to do this work? In some schools the building principal, the literacy coach, and the school secretary work in the building over the summer, so they conduct many of these meetings. At other schools, teachers volunteer to help with one book swap appointment during the summer. If one school is hosting a summer program, then all of the book swap appointments are held at that school.

Schools have found that these book swap appointments are well worth the small investment of time. Many students who typically didn't read over the summer and fell behind in skills now come back to school in the fall reading right where they left off in June.

• Field Trip to the Public Library •

In many school systems, a public librarian visits the schools to talk about the summer reading program. One of our schools found even more success when the class went to the public library. Having a chance to see what the library looked like, searching the bookshelves with their teachers to find their favorite books, and seeing how to get a library card made a difference for many readers.

• Online Book Clubs •

Another motivation for readers to read all summer is class blogs. Before the end of the school year, teachers set up book clubs for their students so that they know what books the class will be blogging about during the summer. Students sign up to read these books and then write a post or comment on each other's posts. Teachers sometimes prepare posts about these books during the school year so during the summer months all they need to do is post what they have written. Connecting students to each other can be very motivating to keep them reading all summer long.

We've Got a Book for That!

Books Organized to Promote Summer Reading

Here are some baskets of books we created with students to support summer reading:

Books Set in Faraway Places

Books Set During the Summer

Authors We Didn't Study This Year

Characters Who Are _____ Graders [upcoming school year]

Books That Make You Laugh

Books That Give Different Perspectives

Adventure Stories

Books You Can Take Home

Books Available at the Public Library

Websites to Read Every Day

If You Liked _____, Then Try _____

Story of a School: Have Books, Will Travel

The Athol-Royalston Elementary Schools wanted to make sure their students had plenty of books to read over the summer. But how could they get books to the students when schools close for these months? To begin, they organized a book swap at each elementary school. The teachers donated extra books from their classrooms and the students brought in books from home. The school district gave each student a drawstring bag to fill with five books to read over the summer.

But there was still a problem. Five books was a good start, but how could they get students enough books to read all summer long? Then the teachers came up with an idea. They knew where many of the kids liked to go in the summer. Many families went to the Salvation Army Summer Fun Club, and other kids attended the summer playground program at the high school. Perhaps they could keep the book swap going all summer long! (See Figure 6.8.)

Once again they asked the community for donations, and the school district ordered even more books. Do you know what happened? Families and kids came to the book swaps, found books they loved, and read all summer long. (See Figure 6.9.)

There's always time for a good

BOOK

at
The Mobile Book Swap!

Dates:
July 7
July 14
July 21
July 28

Figure 6.8: The school sent out bookmarks letting families know when and where they could swap books over the summer.

Figure 6.9: Teachers loaded up their cars and drove books to locations around the town so kids could swap books.

7

Got Books . . . Now What?

Organizing Books to
Support Instruction

If a child leaves us having loved one book,
we have changed the world.

—PERNILLE RIPP

Story of a Reader: If You Like This,
Then You Should Try . . .

Julie notices that Jason is having a difficult time flipping the pages of his book. She points her head in his direction, signaling Tammy's attention. They barely contain their laughter as they see a different book fall out from behind the one he is holding. Jason quickly readjusts so only the poetry book he is "reading" is visible. Julie and Tammy make their way over.

"How's it going, Jason?"

"Great."

"Tell us more about the poems you are reading."

"I like the rhymes. They're good."

"Why don't you read us one you really like?"

At this point the jig is up, and Jason reveals the book on bugs he is reading. "I just don't like poetry," he explains. "Why do I have to read it?"

Julie and Tammy exchange glances and Julie decides to take this one.

"I am sorry to hear you haven't connected with poetry yet. We're studying poetry for this month, so as a reader that is the genre you are getting to know. You can read other genres too, but we want you to give poetry a chance. It is important that readers learn about all kinds of writing and how authors craft those types of writing."

Jason nods and puts his book on bugs into his desk.

"Do you like bugs?" Julie continues.

"I *love* bugs."

"We have a poetry book you are going to love. Let me show you."

Julie brings Jason over to the classroom library and gets the basket of bug books. She searches through the titles and pulls out *Insectlopedia*, by Douglas Florian.

"That's not a poetry book. It is in the Bug Books basket," Jason says.

"It is poetry–poems about bugs."

"I thought all the books in this bin were informational."

"Well, this book does have information about bugs; it is just crafted as poetry."

"Cool! Can I have it?"

"Sure. Let me know what you think when you are done," Julie reminds him.

Julie's knowledge of books transformed a potential power struggle into an exciting new venture. It was a masterful instructional move that was made possible by her knowledge of books.

Fountas and Pinnell (1999) highlight the importance of knowing books.

> Matching books to readers depends on three interrelated sets of understandings, all of which are critical to effective teaching:
> - Knowing the readers.
> - Knowing the texts.
> - Understanding the reading process. (1)

Teachers consider their instructional model, curriculum standards, and text complexity when they choose books, but these considerations mean little if we don't know which actual books meet these considerations. The process of reorganizing our books for the bookroom and our classroom libraries (see Chapters 3 and 4) helps us think about how to use texts to both instruct and engage our students. Grade levels may be assigned certain authors, genres, or topics to study, but teachers ultimately choose the texts they will use. As Fountas and Pinnell suggest, choosing books requires us to think about the reading process, the types of texts we are studying, and the developmental stage of our readers if we want to engage and instruct our students meaningfully and purposefully. Let's start by taking a closer look at how the reading process impacts how we organize books to support our instruction.

Understanding the Reading Process

Research that studied the processes of proficient readers identified a core set of seven strategies readers used to comprehend text (Pearson et al. 1992).

What Strategies Do Readers Use?

- retelling
- schema
- monitoring for meaning
- asking questions
- sensory images
- inferring
- determining importance.

Instructionally, this research plays out for many of us as units of study focused on each comprehension strategy. Many teachers and schools, therefore, organize books by these comprehension strategies—for example, creating baskets of books perfect for teaching schema or sensory images. David Perkins (2009) of Harvard's Project Zero has called this approach "elementitis." Vicki Vinton introduced us to this research in her book *Dynamic Teaching for Deeper Reading* (2017). "When it comes to the teaching of reading, elementitis is at play when we break down the complex process of reading into discrete, separate pieces. We teach strategies, for instance, one at a time, despite the fact that reading for meaning requires using a whole suite of them" (5).

Rumelhart's (1980) interactive reading model, however, focuses on how the cognitive structures in the brain work to make meaning from text. Rumelhart's theory shows that readers actually process using these structures simultaneously. Reading is not a linear process, using one metacognitive strategy, then the next; rather, it's a complex, interactive process that is used to create meaning using various sources of information from the text and the reader's schema simultaneously. So what does this mean for our instruction? How do we use books to teach our students these reading strategies and show them how to use them in a way that reflects an authentic reading process? How does it impact the way we organize the books we use to scaffold our instruction?

We try to find a balance! We still spend some time explicitly teaching each strategy to young learners and choose to slow down and examine one specific strategy when students are having difficulty interacting with the text. We find, however, our instruction has shifted to spending more time showing how the strategies are integrated. When we were solely teaching units that highlighted one particular strategy, we noticed our young readers developing tunnel vision for the new strategy and saying goodbye to strategies we'd previously taught. Students seemed to be viewing strategies as activities to be done with certain books rather than as a metacognitive process they should employ as needed. We don't tuck into bed at night with a book and decide to only make connections with the characters. Our brains do the reading work presented by the text we are reading. Proficient readers are flexible, efficient, and responsive. The use of these strategies develops over time as the reader learns which ones are best matched to the text being read. For us, organizing our units of study and mentor texts solely by comprehension strategy was not supporting the development of proficient, flexible readers. We have changed the way we teach these cognitive structures and have reorganized some of our mentor texts to support this change.

Our units of study are now organized by genre, structure, element, author, topic, and device. We create text sets organized by one of these factors and use these texts to model the reading strategies as we authentically use them. We still model, notice, wonder, and discuss—our teaching is just more flexible and integrated in terms of strategy use. We allow our students' natural use of strategies to guide the modeling we choose to do in our lessons. For example, when the class erupts into laughter as the character from David Shannon's *No, David!*

runs naked down the street, we stop, notice, and name the work they are doing as readers. We point out that they are connecting to the text, having a sensory image, and responding to the character in the book. When they shout out during our read-aloud, telling the characters in the book *One*, by Kathryn Otoshi, what to do, we stop, notice, and name the work they are doing as readers. We show them that they are making text-to-self connections, considering point of view, having sensory images, and empathizing with a character.

The books we choose help us navigate the instructional journey of our units of study. Now, as with all effective teaching, finding the right book to make this happen requires careful, intentional planning. The whole-class section of the bookroom is designed to support finding these books. We organize books by element, device, topic, and so on for any teacher to access as needed throughout the year. The books we use to support our ELA and content curriculum are organized into baskets by units of study for each grade level. (See Figure 7.1.) Some books may still be organized by comprehension strategy for the times when we need a book that is perfectly matched to teaching a particular reading strategy, but most texts are organized by unit of study, literary elements, and devices. Taking the time to organize our books this way not only enhances our teaching but helps us get to know our books better.

Knowing the Books

What's tricky about teaching these cognitive reading strategies is that how they are used depends upon both the developmental stage of the reader (what the reader is ready to do) and the text itself (what the text pushes a reader's brain to do). We need to be aware of both factors—reader and text—when we choose books for instructional purposes. While most books provide opportunities to model most strategies, we do think some books lend themselves to thinking and talking about certain devices, elements, crafts, and structures. Our metacognitive processes naturally focus on particular text elements—who doesn't laugh when Fly Guy buzzes and then is surprised when Buzz answers him?—and as readers we notice the moves of an author and wonder why the author made those moves. When we think about the developmental stages and

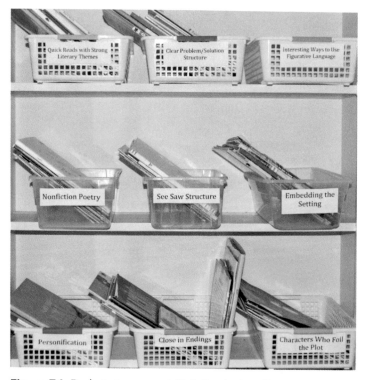

Figure 7.1: Baskets to support ELA Curriculum Content

interests of our readers, we think about which of these elements, devices, and strategies they are ready to explore with us and on their own. Following are some of the resources we rely on when looking for lists of great children's literature to read aloud, study, and use to model (also see OR 7.1 and 7.2).

Professional Books with Lists of Mentor Children's Books

The Art of Teaching Reading, Lucy McCormick Calkins (2001)

Beyond Leveled Books, 2nd ed., Karen Szymusiak and Franki Sibberson (2008)

The Book Whisperer, Donalyn Miller (2009)

Catching Readers Before They Fall, Pat Johnson and Katie Keier (2010)

Mentor Texts, 2nd ed. (2017); *Nonfiction Mentor Texts* (2009); and *Poetry Mentor Texts* (2012), Lynne R. Dorfman and Rose Cappelli

Mosaic of Thought, 2nd ed., Ellin Oliver Keene and Susan Zimmermann (2007)

Reading in the Wild, Donalyn Miller (2014)

Reading with Meaning, Debbie Miller (2012)

Significant Studies for Second Grade, Karen Ruzzo and Mary Anne Sacco (2004)

Strategies that Work, 3rd ed., Anne Goudvis and Stephanie Harvey (2017)

7 Keys to Comprehension, Susan Zimmermann (2003)

Teaching Interpretation: Using Text-Based Evidence to Construct Meaning, Sonja Cherry-Paul and Dana Johansen (2014)

Teaching Reading in Small Groups, Jennifer Serravallo (2010)

Dream Wakers: Mentor Texts that Celebrate Latino Cultures, Ruth Culham (2016)

Craft Moves: Lesson Sets for Teaching Writing with Mentor Texts, Stacey Shubitz (2016)

• Genre and Structure •

Readers think about genre and structure. Randy Bomer reminds us, "Every piece of writing, every text we read, comes to us both as a text—the piece it is—and as a kind of text—an instance of genre. And what kind of thing it is puts some limits as to what we expect to find there. Genre, an often overlooked cueing system in reading, constrains our predictions, and lays down a track for our reading" (1995, 117). When we choose texts, we need to think about what our readers already know about genre and structure and what they are ready to learn next.

We recommend as well that schools create ELA and content curriculum sections of the bookroom where some mentor texts are organized by genre or structure and grade level so it helps teachers know what students have previously experienced. When we know the texts our students have read, it helps us choose our next texts.

PEEK INTO PLANNING

A second-grade team is planning for a unit of study on traditional tales. This will be the third year these students have studied this genre. In kindergarten they studied nursery rhymes and in first grade they studied fairy tales. In second grade they will be studying adapted fairy tales. The teachers want to launch the unit by making connections between the fairy tales the kids studied last year and the adapted fairy tales they will study this year. How are they the same? How are they different? How did the author adapt the tale? Why did the author adapt it in this way? The teachers discuss how they might proceed.

"Here are the mentor texts all the grade 1 teachers used last year. We might want to start the unit by using some of the ones they read last year."

"That makes sense to start with an original they know and then read an adapted version of it. Do we have any adaptations that go with the originals they read in first grade?"

"We do. *The Three Little Pigs, Cinderella, Little Red Riding Hood, Gingerbread Man,* and *Three Billy Goats Gruff* all match the adapted versions we have for mentor texts."

"I am thinking about launching with *Cinderella*. My students are ready to think about the author's big idea and purpose. I have lots of versions of *Cinderella*, so I think it will work well to discuss why the author chose the adaptation he chose. *Cinderella* also has a pretty clear theme or big idea."

"I am thinking of starting with *The Gingerbread Man*. My class is just starting to notice the role setting plays in a story. I have lots of different versions of this story and the setting is different in many of them. I think this will help them think about setting—why an author would choose to change it and how it impacts the story."

The teachers continue to plan the unit of study based on the books in the bookroom and the developmental needs of their students.

Figure 7.2: Choosing mentor texts collaboratively helps us plan vertically.

Here are some suggestions for how to organize books by genre and structure that relate to ELA curriculum:

Genre

Mysteries

Biographies

Song Books

Realistic Fiction

Historical Fiction

Fantasy

Poetry

Traditional Tales

Plays/Dramas

Structure

Compare and Contrast

Narrative Nonfiction

Graphic Novels

Wordless Books

Short Stories

Question-and-Answer Books

Chapters Told from Different Points of View

Journal Entries

Seesaw Structure

See OR 7.3 for a list of specific titles.

• Elements and Devices •

Literary elements are what the text is composed of and literary devices are structures used by authors to convey meaning or a message. We often think of the elements as what the story is about and the devices as the way the author structures the writing. It is not enough for students to just identify the elements and repeat the sequence of the story. Reading in the twenty-first century requires students to think deeply about the elements and how they impact each other. They must also be aware that some texts focus more on certain elements—that is, there are books that have great examples of plot structure and books that really show character development. When we choose texts, we need to think about what our readers know about the elements and devices and what they are ready to learn next. This is an important way to think about book organization from kindergarten on up!

Here are a few ideas for book baskets organized by literary devices and elements. See OR 7.4 for some lists of baskets and books organized by element or device.

Literary Elements

Embedding the Setting

Theme: Acceptance

Theme: Perseverance—Building a Growth Mind-Set

Theme: Kindness

Theme: Overcoming Challenges

Theme: Standing Up for Your Beliefs

Character: Man Versus Nature

Character: Man Versus Man

Character: Man Versus Himself

Character: Character Foils the Plot

Literary Devices

Books that Bring Out a Strong Mood

Personification

Foreshadowing

Flashbacks

Repetition

Rhythm and Rhyme

Simile and Metaphor

Symbolism

Mood

Imagery

Alliteration

PEEK INTO PLANNING

The third-grade team at one school was about to begin a unit of study on mysteries. There are so many great mysteries for this age group and the school had a lot of them organized as a series in the independent reading section of the bookroom.

One teacher explained, "I am worried about this unit of study for my students. They are stuck with only predicting plot, and this genre is going to reinforce this level of comprehension. I want them to read more closely and notice the subtleties of the plot and characters."

"I agree," another replied. "This unit will help them work on reading longer texts and carrying comprehension across a longer text, but it won't challenge them to read beyond surface-level plot."

"They do need to read longer texts, so that is a good thing."

"I love mysteries. I am an avid mystery reader and I don't agree at all. There are many subtleties to a mystery. What about red herrings? We could teach red herrings—that would slow them down to read more closely," a colleague suggested.

"That's a great idea. Do we have any mystery series with red herrings?"

Phil, a third grade teacher, waved the team over to the series baskets in the independent reading section of the bookroom and started to grab baskets of mysteries. "All of these have red herrings," he said. The others looked at the series he'd pulled out.

Cam Jansen

A to Z Mysteries

Clubhouse Mysteries

Jigsaw Jones Mysteries

Nate the Great

High-Rise Private Eyes

Katie Kazoo, Switcheroo

The Chicken Squad

Jack Russell: Dog Detective

Shelter Pet Squad

"Wow, that's a lot," one of the teachers said. "These will be great for them to read in book clubs."

"Is there a more sophisticated mystery we could read for our interactive read-aloud?" another asked.

"Sure. I love *Chasing Vermeer*, Benjamin Pratt and the Keepers of the School, Eddie Red Undercover, and 43 Old Cemetery Road—those are all great for read-aloud. We even have class sets of those in the interactive read-aloud section of the bookroom. I'll grab them!" (See Figures 7.3 and 7.4.)

Figure 7.3: Organizing books for interactive read-aloud

Figure 7.4: Organizing books by series

How Do Mentor Texts Support
Thoughtful Planning?

Lynne Dorfman and Rose Cappelli first defined mentor texts for us in their book *Mentor Texts*: "Mentor texts are pieces of literature that we can return to again and again as we help our young writers learn how to do what they may not yet be able to do on their own" (2017, 2). For us, a mentor text truly becomes an additional teacher in the room. When organizing books in book-rooms and classroom libraries, we find this definition to be very important. Some books may be used to model a lesson or two, but mentor texts are used repeatedly throughout the year. When it comes to books in a shared space like the bookroom that are used to model or study as a whole class, the question of whose book it is comes up. It is often an issue when teachers create baskets of books to model particular strategies or to examine specific elements. Teachers discover that the same books may be used year after year for the same purpose. Many schools debate whether to have books assigned to certain grade levels, meaning only one grade level can read those books. We try to strike a balance by using mentor texts.

During each unit of study for a particular grade level, we assign one to two mentor texts that every student will experience. This provides consistency for the students and flexibility for teachers when choosing the other texts for the unit. When teachers across the grade levels know the books that every student has experienced in every grade level, we can use those texts purposefully. Planning how the mentor texts will support and extend each other as students move through the grades is very powerful.

When we organize our books we look at how our mentor texts connect throughout a year and throughout a K–6 experience. These books journey with our students throughout their elementary school career to reread, dis-cuss, and analyze in relation to other books they are reading. Each year, they reread a book and discover new layers of meaning. These mentor texts serve as teachers who travel with the students. They provide current teachers with a sense of history and a glimpse into the future.

Bookrooms provide a space to plan and share books vertically across grades so students can revisit books and we can introduce new concepts or strategies with books the students have already experienced. While we want to have sections of the bookroom that are grade-level-specific to ensure some novelty each year, we also want to purposefully plan to reread some mentor texts.

Honoring All Readers in the Books We Choose

When we reorganize our books, we want to be mindful that we include books that represent the multiplicity of our world. It is critical that all of our students have the opportunity to see themselves in the books they are choosing *and* to meet characters that are different from themselves. As Chad Everett writes, "Our classroom libraries, (therefore), must contain a variety of texts, allowing each student to read across his or her continuum. All readers should be able to find texts that affirm their lives and experiences. All readers should be able to find texts that affirm the lives and experiences of others" (2017). We believe the best way to do this is to ensure all of our book baskets contain books with a variety of characters across race, class, ethnicity, gender, and orientation, and by including authors from all backgrounds. In JoEllen McCarthy's blog post she reminds us, "As a community of readers, we seek books that encourage unity. We seek books that represent our students, our world and celebrate both. We seek books that encourage students to interact, communicate, connect, work and play together as a community of learners" (2016). Following is a list of a few websites, apps, magazines, and blogs we use to help us curate a book collection that honors all readers (also see OR 7.5).

Finding Books to Support a Diverse Library and Bookroom

- *American Library Association:* ALA's website has links to book, print and media awards as well as book lists of recommended books (Best of . . .) (www.ala.org/awardsgrants/awards/browse /bpma?showfilter=no).

- *Salaam Reads:* The Salaam Reads website lists children's books that feature a wide variety of Muslim children and their families (http://salaamreads.com/phone/index.html).

- *We Need Diverse Books:* The We Need Diverse Books website provides links to lists of diverse titles. You can also use their "Our Story" app to find diverse books. You simply check off what you are interested in finding and the app generates a list of books with diverse content and by authors/illustrators from marginalized communities (http://weneeddiversebooks.org).

- *American Indians in Children's Literature:* This website provides critical insights into the ways that Native peoples are depicted in children's and young adult books. Each November, they award "Best Books" for the year (https://americanindiansin childrensliterature.blogspot.com/p/best-books.html).

- *NCTE Children's Book Awards:* Each November, the NCTE Children's Book Awards are announced. NCTE gives out two awards: the NCTE Charlotte Huck Award for Outstanding Fiction for Children and the Orbis Pictus Award for Outstanding Nonfiction for Children's Literature. Visit www2 .ncte.org/awards/ncte-childrens-book-awards to see the 2017 awards ceremony.

- *The Horn Book:* Six times a year, *The Horn Book Magazine* publishes articles, reviews, and editorials about children's and young adult literature. It is a great way to find out about new titles and read interviews with authors (www.hbook.com /horn-book-magazine-2).

- *A Mighty Girl's Book:* This website features over 2,000 books with strong girl characters. You can sort titles by genre, age group, language, and award winners to help you find just the right books (www.amightygirl.com/books).

- *Grass Roots Community Foundation:* This organization has created a website listing books that feature black girls as main characters. Currently, this website lists over 1,000 titles and this list is

updated each month (http://grassrootscommunityfoundation
.org/1000-black-girl-books-resource-guide).

- *MSU Libraries:* Michigan State University's website has
  an extensive list of award winners and recommended
  diverse children's books (http://libguides.lib.msu.edu
  /c.php?g=96613&p=626686).

- *Guys Read:* This website focuses on books for "guys" of all ages.
  They have book lists organized by topic, author, and genre as well
  as author interviews and audio books (www.guysread.com/books).

Knowing the Reader

There is more to knowing the reader than meets the eye. We need to consider more than text complexity, interest, and stamina when we match books to readers. When we think about the development of our readers we need to think about where they are in the process of learning. Learning requires a person to construct understanding and transfer knowledge and strategy to independent application. The gradual release of responsibility is not only an instructional model but a framework for how we learn. As our students engage in the process of learning new strategies, trying new ways to analyze and respond to text, and reading new structures or genres, we need to think about the types of texts we choose instructionally. Text serves as a scaffold—offering supports or challenges, depending on what the reader needs. When we choose books for our students, we think about how to purposefully use texts as scaffolds to increase or decrease the level of challenge or support. Following are some factors we consider when using text as a scaffold.

• Text Length •

We are always on the lookout for wonderful short texts that we can read aloud. Short texts are succinct models that are perfect for teaching new reading strategies. They also provide options and scaffolds for readers who are trying new structures, an increased level of complexity, sophisticated content, or analysis. The length of a text can support readers as they grow and develop. Short texts allow students to transfer what they have learned to new texts and try it many times, since they can finish them in a short amount of time.

As we watch our children learn how to play baseball or soccer, we hear the coaches telling the kids to "swing" or "get the ball off [their] foot!" Coaches know that the best way to get better at something is to do it more often. The more opportunities you have to swing the bat at the ball, the better your timing, speed, and accuracy will become. The more chances you have to kick the ball into the goal, the better the chance you will score. We believe it is the same with reading: elementary readers need to "take a lot of shots on goal." We want them to see many characters develop throughout a text; ponder many themes and authors' intentions; and determine the resolution of many plots. Short text scaffolds our readers' development since it gives them more opportunities to practice.

See OR 7.6 for a collection of picture books and short texts we love.

· Text Sets ·

A second-grade class recently read *Good Night, Monkey Boy,* by Jarrett Krosoczka. We were discussing the possible themes, the author's style, and how the author uses point of view in this text. During independent reading one day, Jolena tapped Clare on the shoulder. Clare gave her the "do not interrupt" signal and went back to her conference. Jolena tapped again—a bit harder.

"But this is really important. I think I made a set," Jolena implored.

Clare avoided eye contact and continued with her conference while watching Jolena get an index card, tape, and marker. Jolena wrote something on the card and then proceeded to empty out a basket of books in the library. She carefully placed those books on the floor and filled the basket with all the No, David! books, *Knuffle Bunny*, and *Good Night, Monkey Boy*. She taped the card to the basket and went back to independent reading. During the group share, Clare took the opportunity to ask Jolena about the set she wanted to share.

"Well, I decided to start a new set. I read *Knuffle Bunny* today and I decided it has the same theme as the No, David! books and *Good Night, Monkey Boy*, so I put the set together. Look, I put the books in a basket and labeled the theme: Parents Lose It. All the books in this basket will be about when a parent loses it but still loves the kid in the end."

Over the next few weeks many readers added books to this basket. Here are some of the titles the students put in this text set:

- *No, David!* David Shannon
- *David Gets in Trouble*, David Shannon
- *Knuffle Bunny*, Mo Willems
- *When Sophie Gets Angry—Really, Really Angry*, Molly Bang
- *The Boss Baby*, Marla Frazee
- *Harriet, You'll Drive Me Wild!* Marla Frazee
- *No Nap*, Eve Bunting
- *Good Night, Monkey Boy*, Jarrett Krosoczka

These students designed their own inquiry study! As they created this text set, they were constructing a deeper understanding of theme and debating which texts fit the criteria of the set. We observed students referencing the text, citing evidence to support their thinking, and listening to multiple points of view. The discussion of theme they were having was meaningful and purposeful to the students so they were highly engaged in the process of learning. Creating their own text sets became a scaffold for our students to construct an independent understanding of theme. This experience caused us to pause and think about ways to involve our students in the process of reorganizing our books. It is a way for them to practice what they are learning and be active members of our literacy community by helping curate the classroom library. For some ideas for themed text sets created by and with children, see OR 7.7.

• Reading Task •

The standards that students are being held to are much higher today than when we were first teaching, but developmentally children have not changed. If our students need to use deeper structures to comprehend texts, then we must, at times, choose texts in which the surface structure (decoding and stamina) is simpler. Allowing children to focus less on surface structures gives them more cognitive capacity to think and talk deeply around text. If our elementary-age and middle-grade students need to be thinking deeply about theme, character development, author intention, and symbolism, then we need to choose books that support students in doing this type of thinking. Wordless picture books are one type of text that allows students to explore the deeper meanings and craft without having the cognitive demand of decoding the words. For a list of wordless picture books and resources to find supportive visual images, see OR 7.8.

There is important research to support the use of easier texts to teach more complex literary and nonfiction skills and strategies. Allington's research found that children dramatically improved their literacy skills when given materials that they could read easily. Children who were asked to read texts that were difficult actually lost ground as readers (2013).

There is no true endpoint to learning for a lifelong reader. We continue to explore, experience, connect, and stretch ourselves. Our thoughtful and purposeful text choice supports our students' growth and journey toward becoming autonomous members of the literacy club.

Story of a School: What Happened to Readers Workshop?

"Our middle school teachers have asked if they could join your professional development sessions with our elementary staff," Dr. Fortuna, the superintendent of the Hudson School District, tells us. She is concerned about the students moving from the elementary schools to the middle school. The elementary schools use a workshop model and the middle school does not.

She continues, "Students are unhappy. They are asking why they don't have readers workshop in middle school. They are telling their teachers how much they learned and how much they liked reading in elementary school. They miss reading."

We pause, trying to contain our joy at hearing that these students are advocating for their reading lives in school, to figure out how we can be helpful.

"Clare and I are not middle school teachers. We have never taught seventh or eighth grade on a middle school schedule. We are not comfortable facilitating professional development for these grades," Tammy explains.

"I know that and these teachers know that too. They just want to come to listen and learn to see if they can incorporate aspects of readers workshop into their literacy block schedule."

"Maybe we should do some guided visits to upper-elementary classrooms. We could bring them to see it in action and then debrief the experience together. That might be a good place to start before they join sessions with the elementary teachers," Tammy suggests.

Dr. Fortuna smiles. "I think that they will love that."

"As long as they know we don't know exactly how we would do this in seventh and eighth grades. We have some ideas and lots of resources to share with them. We believe it can, and should, work—we just can't speak from experience."

8

Digital Resources
Opening a World of Possibilities

More than a building that houses books and data, the library represents a window to a larger world, the place where we've always come to discover big ideas and profound concepts that help move the American story forward and the human story forward.
—BARACK OBAMA

Story of a Reader: Using Digital Tools to Engage Readers

Oliver dumps the books out of his book bag, looks into the eyes of his third-grade teacher, Patty, and exclaims, "I don't want to read any of these books."

"Can you tell me why?" Patty asks.

"No one else in this class reads books like these. I want to read books like the other kids read."

Patty looks at the books with Oliver's words in mind. Although these books are at Oliver's independent reading level, the illustrations, size, and shape of the texts are different from what other students in the class are reading.

Patty wonders to herself, "What if these books were digital and the size and shape of the text weren't so prominent? Would Oliver be more engaged in reading?"

The next day, Patty approaches Oliver with an iPad in hand.

"I thought about what you said yesterday and about the books you want to read. I wondered if you might be interested in reading on an e-reader. There are four of these in the bookroom we can borrow. Perhaps you and a few other students might be interested in working in a small group to experiment with e-readers. You could all learn how to use an e-reader and then teach the class how to use them."

Patty opens the iPad and shows Oliver the Toon Books website. "What do you think? Would you be interested in reading books like these?"

Oliver looks up and smiles. "I definitely want to do this."

"At the end of our literacy block, let's ask if there are a few other students who might be interested in joining a small group to explore e-readers."

"Yeah! I know lots of kids are going to want to try e-readers."

Oliver, like many other students, wants to read what his classmates are reading. He doesn't want to stand out because of the types of texts he reads, and we don't want the books he currently reads to impact his reading identity negatively. When Oliver looks at the books in his book bag, they represent what he has not yet learned, so he is not motivated to read them. The mismatch between the books he wants to read and his current reading skills puts him at risk of disengaging with reading. Oliver needs to increase the amount he reads in order to progress, but Oliver doesn't want to read the texts he can read independently. Digital resources may be just the answer to maximize access to text Oliver both wants and needs to read. Digital resources have the potential to open up a world of possibilities in literacy.

Teaching Digital Literacy: It's More Than Integrating Technology into the Classroom

We all have students who share Oliver's story in our classrooms and we must find ways to help each one of them become part of the literacy club. Digital reading can be a bridge between a child's strengths, his interests, and his reading development. Digital reading may be an entry point for engaging students in reading, but our work with digital literacy doesn't stop there.

An International Reading Association (IRA) position statement reminds us of our responsibilities to teach digital literacy: "To become fully literate in today's world, students must become proficient in the new literacies of 21st-century technologies. As a result, literacy educators have a responsibility to effectively integrate these new technologies into the curriculum, preparing students for the literacy future they deserve" (2009). Just like books, digital resources are instructional tools we use to help students develop habits and to learn how to navigate both traditional and digital texts.

We see the importance of digital literacy as we reflect on how our own reading habits have changed over the last ten years. We find we use digital tools and read digitally all day long personally and professionally:

- We read and comment on blog posts.
- We read news highlights on our phones.
- We write posts on our blog.
- We skim Twitter for interesting posts about literacy.
- We listen to children's audio books during our commute to work.
- We read and respond to emails.
- We search for information on our laptops.
- We order and send birthday gifts to relatives.
- We read books on our iPads before bed.

And that is all in just one day!

If digital reading is such a big part of our professional and personal lives right now, it's hard to even imagine the ways our students will use digital tools and resources in fifteen years. Digital resources have made accessing information easier—some would argue more interesting—and have expanded our learning community beyond our workplace and neighborhoods. Digital tools help us learn in new ways and we know that helping our students become digitally literate will help prepare them for the future.

So where do digital tools and resources fit into the mix? What do we need? How do we organize for access in our classroom libraries? What goes in the bookroom? How do we use digital resources to help our students develop a reading identity?

• Digital Resources Maximize Access •

When we first thought about using digital devices in classrooms we had no doubt students would be excited about using them, but we wondered, "Do students have access to digital devices at home and at school? Will this benefit them?" Well, according to the research, for some students and some communities, digital devices might be more accessible than traditional books. Sixty-four percent of American adults now own a smartphone of some kind, up from 35 percent in the spring of 2011 (Smith 2015). Scholastic reports that between 2010 and 2014, the portion of children ages 6–8 who reported having read an e-book more than doubled, from 28% to 64%; similarly, the percentage escalated from 22% to 56% for children ages 9–11 (2014). Let's face it, with the trend on the rise, digital reading may increasingly be one of the best ways to get texts into readers' hands both at school and at home.

• Digital Resources Provide More Choice •

Accessing books digitally may be less expensive. The price of a digital text is often less than that of a paper book and the text can be uploaded to multiple devices. You can also borrow digital texts from the public library and load them

Figure 8.1: Many readers choose digital reading and writing in this classroom.

onto multiple devices. This increases a school's or classroom's volume of books—and the opportunity for student choice.

Digital reading also opens up more opportunities for our students to read throughout the day. If students are reading digitally, they have access to the text as long as they have access to a device. (See Figure 8.1 and OR 7.2) Problems of students getting confused because they are reading different books at home and

PEEK INTO DIGITAL POSSIBILITIES: USING E-READERS

When Annie, a principal, wanted to add to her school's collection of small-group texts for book clubs, she decided to purchase six Kindle e-readers instead of buying traditional books. Annie shared the Kindles and her idea with the fifth-grade team of teachers.

"I would like to experiment with using Kindles as a way to give students access to multiple copies of texts for book clubs. Since I bought six Kindles, under one account I can purchase one copy of a book and load it on all six devices. This way, students can either choose from the books we have in the small-group section of the bookroom or the books we have available digitally. They can also choose any book, with your guidance, and then we can purchase it digitally for them. It will open up possibilities and be less expensive. I know book clubs are really popular, and I want to find the best way to keep our book supply updated. Do you think there is a group of students who might be interested in trying this?"

Every teacher on the team raised her hand.

"Why don't you choose a few students who have not been thrilled with their book club selections lately? Perhaps they would be the best students to try this out."

at school can be reduced with digital reading, when they can access the same book on devices in both places. Problems with students not having books to read over vacations can also be reduced. If we show students in school how to read digitally, we provide opportunities for them to read on their own time. For a list of some of our favorite free digital resources, see OR 8.1.

Buyer Beware

According to Amazon, sometimes publishers limit how many devices can share one book. On average, Amazon says, you can purchase one copy of a book and load it onto six devices.

PEEK INTO DIGITAL POSSIBILITIES: USING DIGITAL BINS

Rose knew that her curriculum standards required fourth graders to read 50 percent literary texts and 50 percent informational texts in school. As she looked at her classroom library, she realized that she didn't have enough interesting informational texts to bring these statistics to life. Rose decided to increase the volume of informational texts by using digital resources. Here is how she introduced this process to her students.

"Each day, before I come to work, I do some informational reading. I skim the headlines in the newspaper on my laptop and choose some interesting articles to read. I read current events and even check the weather. As I was reading this morning, I thought of all of you and how you might also enjoy beginning the day with some informational reading. I was wondering what you might think about foregoing our typical morning work for the next week and reading informational text on digital devices to begin our day."

Cheers erupted in the room.

"Yes! I can't believe it!"

"That is my favorite kind of reading."

"I never thought we were going to be able to do this at school."

Rose continued, "Between the school laptops and the Chromebooks, we have enough devices to try this. I created a digital bin of websites for you to explore. Since this is new, let's work with partners. This will allow you to talk with each other about what you are learning and how digital reading is similar to and different from reading books."

"Can we also explore these websites independently?" John asked.

"Yes, as soon as we learn how to access the websites and get more familiar with digital reading."

We learned about digital bins from Sonja Cherry-Paul and Dana Johansen at a conference. Since then we refer to their book *Teaching Interpretation* (2014) and their blog, *LitLearnAct* (https://litlearnact.wordpress.com/sample-digital-bin), to get new ideas. For more information about how to create digital bins and QR codes, see OR 8.3. See Figure 8.2 and OR 8.2 for a list of online resources with great informational texts for kids.

These informational reading websites are filled with articles, interviews, and videos for students to access. They are updated daily and there is no charge for all or most of the content. On some sites you need to open an account (free of charge), and on others you can simply click and begin reading.

- *Wonderopolis* (http://wonderopolis.org): Each day Wonderopolis posts and answers a new question. From "What does it mean to stand for something?" to "How many eyes does a spider have?" readers can read the daily question or search to find answers to their own questions.

- *DogoNews* (www.dognews.com): This site is filled with articles and videos about current events, sports, and human-interest stories. Dogo also has sites for book and movie reviews—DogoBooks (www.dogobooks.com) and DogoMovies (www.dogomovies.com).

- *Sports Illustrated Kids* (www.sikids.com): Students can read about their favorite sports and sports teams. They can sort articles by the type of sport or read the articles and videos written by kid reporters.

- *Newsela* (https://newsela.com): This website is filled with informational texts for students to explore. We love the way this website organizes information. You can search by topic-based text sets, find primary sources, listen to speeches, and more. In order to access the material you must set up an account, but the good news is that your account is free.

- *Time for Kids* (www.timeforkids.com): There are many free articles about current events on this website. The articles are organized just as in the print magazine ("Latest," "World," "Nation," "Science," "Entertainment," "Health," and "Sports").

Figure 8.2: Digital bin of informational websites for students

• Digital Resources Provide a Broader • Range of Text Complexity

When we taught first and second grades, digital texts were not an option in the classroom. So what did we do when we needed more options for our early and emergent readers? We wrote them ourselves. We took photos of students, glued them on paper, and wrote the words to match. Yes, we had to get the film developed. Yes, it took hours. And yes, we are that old. Thank goodness for digital tools. They have made creating texts to add to our classroom library so much easier. See Figure 8.3 and QR 8.4 for some of our favorite sites for finding texts at a variety of levels.

Here are a few digital resources we use when we are looking for text at an easier range of complexity. These sites have high-interest texts at a variety of levels so students can find texts they can read.

- *ReadWorks* (www.readworks.org): This site is filled with fiction and informational texts for students to read. The way this website is organized makes it easy for teachers to find the texts they need. You can sort by content-area topic (science or social studies), grade level, and Lexile level. You will need to set up a free account to access the material on this website.

- *Toon Books* (www.toon-books.com): This website gives readers access to easy-to-read comics. The comics are organized by grade level and some titles are available in Spanish. Students can not only read comics but also create their own comics (under the "Just for Kids" drop-down menu).

- *PebbleGo* (www.pebblego.com): Franki Sibberson introduced us to this resource. PebbleGo is filled with easy-to-read informational resources students can use to research topics of interest. The texts are organized by topic and level so it is easy to find texts that students are interested in reading and can read. Users must pay a subscription fee in order to access this website.

- *Explorer Magazine* by *National Geographic* (www.nationalgeograph ic.org/education/explorer-magazine): We love the way the National Geographic Society writes its *Explorer* magazines at two different levels. The photographs in the magazines are the same, but the text is different. In order to get these magazines online or in print, users must pay a subscription fee.

Figure 8.3: Incorporating digital resources into the classroom library to provide a broader range of text complexity

PEEK INTO DIGITAL POSSIBILITIES: SUPPORTING EMERGENT READERS

Sarah, a first grader, was more interested in just about anything other than reading. Sarah loved her family, she loved collecting and stuffing pebbles in her socks, and she loved telling stories about her dog. Her teacher, Brian, knew that if he was going to teach Sarah to read, he was going to need to engage her—really engage her. So Brian created books about what she loved most—her life.

He asked Sarah, "Would you like to read a book about you?"

"Yes, that would be cool."

"Great! You can help me make it."

They snapped pictures of Sarah, her rocks, and her classmates. He inserted the photos into PowerPoint and showed them to Sarah.

"Sarah, what do you see in this picture?" he asked, pointing at the first photo.

As Sarah talked, Brian typed, and together they created books that she could read digitally on her own. Later, as Brian watched Sarah read independently, he saw her stopping at each page, reading the words, and laughing.

This worked well as a start, but when funds were available, Brian's school purchased Pioneer Valley's BookBuilder software (see www.bookbuilderonline.com). This software instantly creates books that include a student's name as well as the names of family members, friends, and even pets.

Using Digital Resources to Enhance Instruction and Engagement

In the book *Amplify: Digital Teaching and Learning in the K–6 Classroom*, Katie Muhtaris and Kristin Ziemke remind us, "It's not the tools, it's what we do with it that counts" (2015, 13). They encourage teachers to balance online reading with printed text. "Digital text does affect the physical act of reading: the clarity of the words on the screen, the presence of hyperlinks, and how quickly one can navigate the material impact the reading experience" (46). We know this about ourselves as digital readers. When we read online, we sometimes get distracted by skimming, scanning, and hyperlinking, rather than slowing down and reading closely. As digital readers, students need to know how to apply what they know about reading books when reading digital texts. They also need to learn how to synthesize information across multiple sources when reading digitally. Just as with any book, digital text is our instructional tool to develop and engage our readers.

PEEK INTO DIGITAL POSSIBILITIES: SCAFFOLDING COMPREHENSION

Chrissy's fifth graders are studying literary themes and point of view. The teachers have created a basket in the bookroom to support this curricular unit of study. The basket contains picture books, short texts, poems, and chapter books. It also has a QR code that organizes digital resources such as songs and video clips for the teachers to use instructionally. Using a variety of texts for modeling scaffolds students as they develop a deep understanding of universal themes in literature and how authors can use point of view to bring these themes to life.

Chrissy develops students' understanding of literary theme and point of view by launching this unit with digital media: a video. The students watch a three-minute clip and analyze it together. She has chosen a clip from the Pixar short film *Piper*, easily accessed online.

After watching, they explore many questions together:

- What is the lesson the main character learns? How do you know?
- How does point of view impact the theme?
- How does point of view impact character motivation?
- How do the characters change throughout the video?
- What do you think the theme is? What message is the author sending?

As students discuss their thoughts and refer to the video to support their thinking, they make connections to literary themes and share ideas about how point of view impacts the theme of this video. They even discuss how the message might be different depending on the age of the reader.

"Readers, the work you just did to understand the deeper meanings in that video is exactly what you need to do to uncover the deeper meanings in text. Over the next few weeks, we are going to think more about how authors use literary devices such as point of view to bring out layers of meaning in a text. Remember, the thinking we did to understand this video is the same process we use when we read text."

By initially exploring universal themes and point of view in a modality that is familiar to the students (video),

Chrissy has helped them deepen their understanding about themes and point of view and think about how authors use literary devices to add layers of meaning to a text. With this initial understanding in place and the students' excitement heightened, Chrissy borrows additional baskets from the bookroom organized by literary theme for her students to read and explore independently and in small groups. She has made sure to create QR codes and include them in the baskets so that students can independently access the related videos. For a list of these theme baskets, see OR 8.5.

Practicing Reading Strategies in the Context of Digital Reading

Digital reading is a different kind of reading for all of us—and if we are going to include these resources in our libraries, it's important to teach students how to use the strategies we are teaching them in both print books and digital resources. We know one second-grade teacher, Gina, who decided to purchase an online version of a magazine subscription for her class so that she could show students how to apply the reading strategies they were learning when reading digitally. She noticed that sometimes students weren't transferring their decoding strategies to their digital reading, so she projected a page of text from the online magazine on the interactive whiteboard and modeled how she slows down at unfamiliar words and rereads to problem solve, and then she invited the students to give it a go. By incorporating digital texts into her lessons, Gina helped students internalize and solidify their use of reading strategies. Gina knows that when students learn a reading strategy, they need to know how to employ the strategy flexibly and responsively. Reading digitally helps students transfer learning to multiple contexts.

PEEK INTO DIGITAL POSSIBILITIES: SUPPORTING TEST PREPARATION

"Did you hear the news? Students in grade 4 are required to take the state test online this year!"

"What?!"

The news was a like a fifty-pound weight being passed from teacher to teacher on this fourth-grade team:

"How are our students going to read on a computer?"

"They don't even know how to type."

"How will they know how to navigate through the test?"

"Why is the state doing this?"

Teaching students to navigate the state test was not new to this fourth-grade team. For the past several years, these teachers had spent a few weeks before the state test helping students understand the genre of test taking, showing students how to apply what they had learned when taking a test, and sharing test-taking strategies. They had all of the materials from past years organized and ready to go:

- photocopies of practice items
- student writing exemplars
- baskets of short text organized in the bookroom— short stories, plays, traditional tales, poetry, and informational texts.

After a few moments, Ellen looked at her teammates and said, "How are we going to approach this? The kids will need to practice test-taking strategies and learn how to read online."

Jennifer suggested, "We can still use our baskets of short text, but we will need to add more digital texts. What if we organize some digital texts and practice materials online? We can bookmark the websites students can read to make the process simpler. We can bookmark the practice test sites and digital texts they can read online."

After a bit of research, Jennifer approached her team with the Symbaloo board she had created. "Look at this! I bookmarked all of the websites on this board so it is easy for students to access. All they need to do is click on the tile, and the website opens. They won't have to type in long URLs or search the Web."

"Let's give it a try in our classrooms and see what happens."

Later that week, Ellen shared her thoughts at a team meeting. "You know, the kids are more invested this year than ever before. They love working on the Chromebooks."

Jennifer added, "I have noticed the same thing. They really enjoy reading online and are navigating through the sites easily. Several of my students are even reading these websites at home during their free time. I think we should integrate digital reading into independent reading all year."

• Sparking Inquiry •

There is nothing quite like inquiry to propel a reader and there is nothing like a digital bin to spark it! Digital bins are somewhat like those "make your own adventure" games where you decide what to do or where to go next. Digital bins allow a reader to branch out into new lines of inquiry in response to the questions and interests he has on a topic. We see this happen even when the topic is assigned in a curricular study. Once research on a topic begins, readers ask questions and search the digital bin for resources to help them investigate further. Teachers can design digital bins to promote inquiry and purposefully provide opportunities for a broad range of study on a topic. For example, we know a third-grade classroom where students were studying forces of motion in science. The teacher gathered all the baskets on forces of motion for his grade level from the bookroom and added these baskets to his library. In addition, he created a digital bin for students to explore at the beginning of the unit. For a sample digital bin on forces and motion, see OR 8.6.

• Promoting Response •

Teachers can also use digital tools to provide different, potentially more engaging ways for students to respond to and connect with text. For example, when Rebecca Mealey, a second-grade teacher, noticed her students seemed to be in a rut with their conversations about text, we suggested using a digital tool, Padlet, to lift the quality of their conversations. She created a Padlet board for her interactive read-aloud text, *Boy in the Doghouse*, by Betsy Duffy. She decided to introduce the tool during her read-aloud so she could model how to use it and monitor its effectiveness. Throughout the text, she stopped so students could turn and talk with their partners. She then invited students to synthesize their conversation and add an idea to the Padlet board. She modeled how to use the speech-to-text function to make it easy for students to record their responses. In doing this, Rebecca demonstrated to her students that readers share ideas and theories about a text with each other. This not only helps readers understand each other's perspectives but also often helps us understand the text in a new way. (See Figure 8.4.)

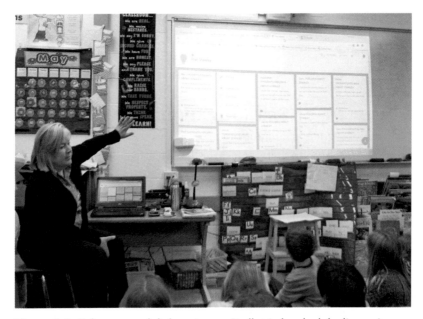

Figure 8.4: Rebecca models how to use Padlet in book club discussions.

Padlet is a great tool for book clubs as well; you can create a Padlet board for each student in a book club so that they can all post questions and respond to each other. It's best when this tool is used to authentically respond to each other and to fuel book club conversations. Students can also sort responses and then use categories they come up with to focus their book club conversations.

Another tool that supports rich response to text is voice notes. Some students—and even some adults—are able to generate and synthesize ideas more readily when speaking them aloud. We've experimented with using voice notes in classrooms to offer another way for students to capture their ideas and grow their thinking about books. And then we created QR codes for the recordings and added those to relevant book baskets in the classroom library and bookroom. We even used some as reviews to advertise books to other readers.

PEEK INTO DIGITAL POSSIBILITIES: PROMOTING CONVERSATION AND DEBATE

Kristen's fifth graders previewed a stack of books and then watched book trailers to determine which books they wanted to read for their upcoming book clubs.

"Ms. C., did you know there is different music in book trailers about the same book?" one student observed.

"I have never thought about the music in the book trailers, but I think you are onto something important. As you are watching book trailers, you can record your ideas about how the music impacts your thoughts about the book. I wonder if the music is related to the reader's interpretation of the book's mood. You know, one of our instructional goals this year is to learn more about the literary devices mood and tone. I think we can use what you have noticed about book trailers to help us with this work. Let's compare and contrast the music in these book trailers with the mood of the book and see if it impacts your opinion," Ms. C. answered.

Using a digital resource, book trailers, helped students choose books and created an opportunity for students to discuss how the music set a tone or mood for the book. Now, as students read, they could consider whether a book trailer accurately depicted the mood of the book, thinking about the following questions.

- Was the mood in the book trailer and in the book the same or different? What makes you think that?
- How did the author's word choice impact the mood of the text?
- How did the choice of music impact the mood of the trailer?
- What music do you think reflects the mood of your book?
- How do you think adding music to the book trailer impacts the review and your opinion of the book?
- Do you think book trailers should have music?

For a specific list of what Kristen included in her literary craft basket on how writers convey mood and tone, see OR 8.7.

• Supporting Revision •

Mentor texts are always in use when students are writing. These texts help students study craft and experiment with revising their writing. Classroom libraries and bookrooms have baskets of texts organized by craft for students to access (see Chapter 3, Figures 3.6 and 3.15.) Recently, we have been using digital bins to organize mentor texts by craft. It is so easy for students to scan a QR code or open a digital bin to find professional, student, and teacher writing samples to study. We also love how easy it is for students to add samples they find helpful to the digital bins. See OR 8.8 for sample mentor text baskets with digital resources.

Sometimes we also use video or podcasts as mentor texts for students to study craft. TED Talks are a favorite for opinion and informational writing. One fourth-grade teacher, Megan, showed her students Sam Berns' poignant TED Talk (www.youtube.com/watch?v=36mlo-tM05g) to help them think about ways to add voice to their informational writing and presentations. After discussing this poignant video, students watched it several times and recorded the craft moves they noticed. As they created their speeches, they tried to incorporate what they had learned from Sam.

Mentor texts can be used to help students revise the notes they take on the books they are reading. So many students in grades 3–6 are now using digital tools to take notes and respond about their reading that we created digital mentor texts for students to study as they draft and revise notes. Students peek into these digital mentor texts to see how readers take notes and write about their reading in authentic ways. We decided to use our own reading notebooks to create digital mentor texts for note taking and reading response. We shared our process with students to give them a glimpse into how we take notes and use them to write blog posts, give book talks, and prepare for book club conversations. To see our first stab at creating a digital mentor text of an annotated reading response for the book *A Handful of Stars*, see OR 8.9.

Story of a School: Digital Resources Ensure No Child Is Excluded from the Literacy Club

We saw Grant sitting by himself while his book club was meeting in the hallway. We decided to check in with him.

"Hey, Grant, we noticed you are not meeting with your book club. What's up?"

"I didn't do the reading. So I can't join. I am trying to catch up now."

We waited.

He continued, "I can't get the reading done. I don't have time. I'm on the bus for two hours every day going to and from Boston for school. I get carsick so I can't read. Plus it's dark, so I can't see anyway. By the time I get home, I barely have time to do my homework and my reading."

Grant was a Boston resident and was in a voluntary program intended to expand educational opportunities, increase diversity, and reduce racial isolation, by permitting students in certain cities to attend public schools in other communities that had agreed to participate. His story stopped us in our tracks. We realized we were missing a huge opportunity to connect students in similar situations with texts. They had all of that time on the bus; we just needed to get them access to texts. We asked Grant to give us some time to come up with some possibilities.

After some research, we wrote a grant to our school foundation and purchased some iPods. These devices allowed us load audio texts so students like Grant could *listen* to books on the bus. We still had print versions of these texts for students to annotate or follow along with if they were able.

Before launching this work, we needed to do some on-the-ground research. "Grant, we have an idea and we need your help," we told him.

We rode the bus to Boston and back with Grant for a few weeks to work out the logistics. He was our ambassador, happy to help others learn how to use the devices and willing to help us take care of them. Grant even organized book clubs on the bus—and we were lucky enough to join a few.

EPILOGUE

An ideal education system is not required before all children can be introduced into the literacy club. Certainly more might be done educationally and politically to recognize the importance of the club and the futility of programmatic instruction. But even given schools as they are, there should always be room for teachers to expand the activities of the literacy clubs, in which all children have an opportunity to engage with more experienced members in productive and rewarding reading and writing activities, in classrooms and outside. The overriding concern must always be that no child is excluded. (Smith 1988, 16)

It is hard to believe that Frank Smith wrote these words in 1988 and they still ring true today. We need to work together to advocate for all children to have access to the literacy club. Books and digital resources make this possible. We *know* it's possible because we observe teachers and librarians welcoming students into the literacy club each and every day. Now it is time to make sure teachers and librarians have the tools they need—books and digital resources—to make this ethical, civic responsibility a reality for every child, in every school, every day. Donalyn Miller reminds us, "Teaching our students to be wild readers is not only possible; it is our ethical responsibility as reading teachers and lifelong readers. Our students deserve it, society demands it, and our teaching hearts know that it matters" (2014, xxiv).

We want this book to impact the lives of teachers and students directly, so we are donating all royalties it generates to the Book Love Foundation. Book Love is a nonprofit organization founded by Penny Kittle with one goal: to put books in the hands of teenagers. Our book will now expand that goal and put books into the hands of elementary and middle-grade students as well. Thank you, Penny, for allowing us to bring the heart of this book to life through your hard work and vision.

When you stop to think about what is possible, it is easy to see the impact you can make. We did! "Each little thing we do goes out, like a ripple, into this world. Even small things count" (Woodson 2012, 20). Thank you for joining us in making a ripple in the life of a child by buying this book; we just took one step toward ensuring all students have equal access to the books they need to become lifelong readers.

WORKS CITED

Allington, Richard L. 2000. *What Really Matters for Struggling Readers: Designing Research-Based Programs*. Boston: Allyn and Bacon.

———. 2002. "What I've Learned About Effective Reading Instruction from a Decade of Studying Exemplary Classroom Teachers." *The Phi Delta Kappan* 83 (10): 740–47. https://diywithrti.files.wordpress.com/2013/05/what-ive-learned-about-effective-reading-instruction.pdf.

———. 2013. "What Really Matters When Working with Struggling Readers." *The Reading Teacher* 66 (7): 520–30. www.ocmboces.org/tfiles/folder1237/1603_Allington _WRM.RT_.pdf.

Allington, Richard L., and Rachael E. Gabriel. 2012. "Every Child, Every Day." *Educational Leadership* 69 (6): 10–15. www.ascd.org/publications/educational-leader ship/mar12/vol69/num06/Every-Child,-Every-Day.aspx.

Allington, Richard, and Anne McGill-Franzen. 2009. "Why Summers Matter in the Rich/Poor Achievement Gap." *Teachers College Record*. ID number: 15757. www .researchgate.net/profile/Anne_Mcgill-Franzen/publication/267687109_Why _Summers_Matter_in_the_RichPoor_Achievement_Gap/links/546df32b0cf23 fe753da809c.pdf.

Barnhouse, Dorothy. 2014. *Readers Front and Center: Helping All Students Engage with Complex Texts*. Portland, ME: Stenhouse.

Barnhouse, Dorothy and Vicki Vinton. 2012. *What Readers Really Do: Teaching the Process of Meaning Making*. Portsmouth, NH: Heinemann.

Betts, E.A. 1946. *Foundations of Reading Instruction: With Emphasis on Differentiated Guidance*. New York: American.

Bishop, Rudine Sims. 1990. "Mirrors, Windows, and Sliding Glass Doors." *Perspectives: Choosing and Using Books for the Classroom* 6 (3): ix–xi.

Black, Paul, and Dylan William. 1998. *Inside the Black Box: Raising Standards Through Classroom Assessment*. Arlington, VA: Phi Delta Kappa International.

Bomer, Randy. 1995. *Time for Meaning: Crafting Literate Lives in Middle and High School*. Portsmouth, NH: Heinemann.

Calkins, Lucy McCormick. 2001. *The Art of Teaching Reading*. New York: Longman.

———. 2006. *A Guide to the Writing Workshop, Grades 3–5*. Portsmouth, NH: FirstHand.

Calkins, Lucy, Norah Mallaney, Shana Frazin, and Colleagues. 2016. *A Guide to the Teachers College Reading and Writing Project Classroom Libraries: Grades 3–5*. Portsmouth, NH: Heinemann.

Calkins, Lucy, Alexandra Marron, and Colleagues from the Teachers College Reading and Writing Project. 2015. *Reading Pathways, Performance Assessments and Learning Progressions: Grades 3–5*. Portsmouth, NH: Heinemann.

Campuzano, Larissa, Mark Dynarski, Roberto Agodini, and Kristina Rall. 2009. "Effectiveness of Reading and Mathematics Software Products Findings from Two Student Cohorts." NCEE 2009-4042. Washington, DC: National Center for Education Evaluation and Regional Assistance, Institute of Education Sciences, U.S. Department of Education. ies.ed.gov/ncee/pubs/20094041/pdf/20094042.pdf.

CBS News. 2016. "Traveling School Librarian Spreads Enthusiasm for Reading." CBSNews.com, April 16. Accessed July 14, 2017. www.cbsnews.com/news/traveling -school-librarian-john-schumacher-spreads-enthusiasm-for-reading/.

Cherry-Paul, Sonja, and Dana Johansen. 2014. *Teaching Interpretation: Using Text-Based Evidence to Construct Meaning*. Portsmouth, NH: Heinemann.

———. 2017. *LitLearnAct* (blog). https://litlearnact.wordpress.com.

Culham, Ruth. 2016. *Dream Wakers: Mentor Texts that Celebrate Latino Cultures*. Portland, ME: Stenhouse.

Cunningham, Anne E., and Keith E. Stanovich. 1998. "The Impact of Print Exposure on Word Recognition." In *Word Recognition in Beginning Literacy*, edited by Jamie L. Matsala and Linne C. Ehri, 235–62. Mahwah, NJ: Lawrence Erlbaum.

Cunningham, Patricia Marr, and Richard L. Allington. 1999. *Classrooms that Work: They Can All Read and Write*. Boston: Pearson.

Dorfman, Lynne R., and Rose Cappelli. 2009. *Nonfiction Mentor Texts: Teaching Informational Writing Through Children's Literature, K–8*. Portland, ME: Stenhouse.

———. 2012. *Poetry Mentor Texts: Making Reading and Writing Connections, Grades K–8*. Portland, ME: Stenhouse.

———. 2017. *Mentor Texts: Teaching Writing Through Children's Literature, K–6*. 2nd ed. Portland, ME: Stenhouse.

Edwards, Carolyn P., Lella Gandini, and George Forman, editors. 1998. *The Hundred Languages of Children: The Reggio Emilia Approach—Advanced Reflections*. 2nd ed. Westport, CT: Ablex.

Ehri, Linnea C., Lois G. Dreyer, Bert Flugman, Alan Gross. 2007. "Reading Rescue: An Effective Tutoring Intervention Model for Language-Minority Students Who Are Struggling Readers in First Grade." *American Educational Research Journal* 44 (2): 414–448.

Everett, Chad. 2017. "There is No Diverse Book." *Imaginelit* (blog), November 21. www.imaginelit.com/news/2017/11/21/there-is-no-diverse-book.

Farstrup, Alan E., and S. Jay Samuels. 2002. *What Research Has to Say About Reading Instruction*. 3rd ed. Newark, DE: International Reading Association.

Fountas, Irene, and Gay Su Pinnell. 1996. *Guided Reading: Good First Teaching for All Children*. 2nd ed. Portsmouth, NH: Heinemann.

———. 1999. *Matching Books to Readers: Using Leveled Books in Guided Reading, K–3*. Portsmouth, NH: Heinemann.

———. 2005. *Leveled Books, K–8: Matching Texts to Readers for Effective Teaching*. Portsmouth, NH: Heinemann.

———. 2012. "Progress Monitoring by Instructional Text Reading Level." Portsmouth, NH: Heinemann. www.heinemann.com/fountasandpinnell/supportingmaterials /bas/10monthprogressbyinstructionallevel.pdf.

Gallagher, Kelly. 2009. *Readicide: How Schools Are Killing Reading and What We Can Do About It*. Portland, ME: Stenhouse.

Gladwell, Malcolm. 2000. *The Tipping Point: How Little Things Can Make a Big Difference*. Boston: Little, Brown.

Goudvis, Anne, and Stephanie Harvey. 2017. *Strategies that Work: Teaching Comprehension for Engagement, Understanding, and Building Knowledge*. 3rd ed. Portland, ME: Stenhouse.

Guthrie, John T., and Allan Wigfield. 1997. "Relations of Children's Motivation for Reading to the Amount and Breadth of Their Reading." *The Journal of Educational Psychology* 89 (3): 420–432.

Guthrie, John T., Allan Wigfield, Nicole M. Humenick, Kathleen C. Perencevich, Ana Taboada, and Pedro Barbosa. 2006. "Influences of Stimulating Tasks on Reading Motivation and Comprehension." *The Journal of Educational Research* 99 (4): 232–45. www.cori.umd.edu/research-publications/2006-guthrie-wigfield-hum.pdf.

Hack, C., S. Hepler, and J. Hickman. 1993. *Children's Literature in the Elementary School*, 5th edition. New York: Holt, Rinehart & Winston.

International Reading Association (IRA). 1999. *Excellent Reading Teachers: A Position Statement of the International Reading Association*. Newark, DE: IRA. www.literacyworld wide.org/docs/default-source/where-we-stand/excellent-reading-teachers-position -statement.pdf?sfvrsn=6.

International Reading Association (IRA). 2009. *New Literacies and 21st-Century Technologies: A Position Statement of the International Reading Association*. Newark, DE: IRA. www.literacyworldwide.org/docs/default-source/where-we-stand/new-literacies -21st-century-position-statement.pdf?sfvrsn=6.

Ivey, Gay, and Peter Johnston. 2013. "Engagement with Young Adult Literature: Outcomes and Processes." *Reading Research Quarterly* 48 (3): 255–75.

Jackson, Andrew P., et al., eds. 2012. *The 21st-Century Black Librarian in America: Issues and Challenges*. Toronto: Scarecrow.

Johnson, Pat, and Katie Keier. 2010. *Catching Readers Before They Fall: Supporting Readers Who Struggle, K–4*. Portland, ME: Stenhouse.

Keene, Ellin Oliver, and Susan Zimmermann. 2007. *Mosaic of Thought: Teaching Comprehension in a Reader's Workshop*. 2nd ed. Portsmouth, NH: Heinemann.

Kittle, Penny. 2013. *Book Love: Developing Depth, Stamina, and Passion in Adolescent Readers*. Portsmouth, NH: Heinemann.

Krashen, Stephen. 1997–98. "Bridging Inequity with Books." *Educational Leadership* 55 (4): 18–22. www.ascd.org/publications/educational-leadership/dec97/vol55/num04/Bridging-Inequity-With-Books.aspx.

———. 2000. *Has Whole Language Failed?* Los Angeles: Center for Multilingual Multicultural Research.

———. 2004. *The Power of Reading: Insights from the Research*. 2nd ed. Portsmouth, NH: Heinemann.

———. 2011. *Free Voluntary Reading*. Santa Barbara, CA: Libraries Unlimited.

Lipski, Frank. 2013. "Create QR Codes and Short Links Using Google Drive." YouTube video, May 25. www.youtube.com/watch?v=bkFe94_hyuY.

Lyengar, Sunil, and Dana Giola. 2007. *To Read or Not to Read: A Question of National Consequence*. Research Report 47. Washington, DC: National Endowment for the Arts. www.arts.gov/sites/default/files/ToRead.pdf.

McCarthy, JoEllen. 2016. "It's the Most Wonderful Time of the Year." *Heinemann Blog* (blog), October 3. https://blog.heinemann.com/wonderful-time-year.

McCarthy, JoEllen. 2017. "Choosing Books." NCTE Conference, St. Louis, MO, November 16–19. https://padlet.com/McCarthyPD/NCTE17.

McQuillan, Jeff. 1998. *The Literacy Crisis: False Claims and Real Solutions*. Portsmouth, NH: Heinemann.

Miller, Debbie. 2012. *Reading with Meaning: Teaching Comprehension in the Primary Grades*. 2nd ed. Portland, ME: Stenhouse.

Miller, Donalyn. 2009. *The Book Whisperer: Awakening the Inner Reader in Every Child*. San Francisco: Jossey-Bass.

———. 2014. *Reading in the Wild: The Book Whisperer's Keys to Cultivating Lifelong Reading Habits*. San Francisco: Jossey-Bass.

———. 2017. "On the Level." *Nerdy Book Club* (blog), October 15. https://nerdybookclub.wordpress.com/2017/10/15/on-the-level-by-donalyn-miller.

Muhtaris, Katie, and Kristin Ziemke. 2015. *Amplify: Digital Teaching and Learning in the K–6 Classroom*. Portsmouth, NH: Heinemann.

National Council of Teachers of English (NCTE). 2017. "Statement on Classroom Libraries." May 31. Accessed July 14, 2017. www.ncte.org/positions/statements /classroom-libraries.

National Governors Association (NGA) Center for Best Practices and Council of Chief State School Officers (CCSSO). 2010. "English Language Arts Standards." In *Common Core State Standards*. Washington, DC: NGA Center for Best Practices and CCSSO. www.corestandards.org/ELA-Literacy.

Neuman, Susan B. 2005. *The Importance of the Classroom Library*. New York: Scholastic. http://teacher.scholastic.com/products/paperbacks/downloads/library.pdf.

Parrott, Kiera. 2017. "Fountas and Pinnell Say Librarians Should Guide Readers by Interest, Not Level." *School Library Journal*, October 12. www.slj.com/2017/10/literacy /fountas-pinnell-say-librarians-guide-readers-interest-not-level.

Pearson, P. David, and M. C. Gallagher. 1983. "The Instruction of Reading Comprehension." *Contemporary Educational Psychology* 8 (3): 317–44.

Pearson, P. David, Laura R. Roehler, Janice A. Dole, and Gerald G. Duffy. 1992. "Developing Expertise in Reading Comprehension: What Should Be Taught? How Should It Be Taught?" In *What Research Has to Say to the Teacher of Reading*, 2nd ed., edited by S. Jay Samuels and Alan E. Farstrup, 1–39. Newark, DE: International Reading Association.

Perkins, David. 2009. *Making Learning Whole: How Seven Principles of Teaching Can Transform Education*. San Francisco: Jossey-Bass.

Recht, Donna R., and Lauren Leslie. 1988. "Effect of Prior Knowledge on Good and Poor Readers' Memory of Text." *Journal of Educational Psychology* 80 (1): 16–20.

Ripp, Pernille. 2017. "Passionate Readers: The Art of Reaching and Engaging Every Child." Speech presented at nErDcampMI, Western High School, Parma, Michigan, July 10.

Roberts, Kate, and Maggie Beattie Roberts. 2016. *DIY Literacy: Teaching Tools for Differentiation, Rigor, and Independence*. Portsmouth, NH: Heinemann.

Rosenblatt, L. M. 1983. *Literature as Exploration*, 4th edition. New York: Modern Language Association. Originally published 1938 by MLA.

———. 1978. *The Reader, the Text, the Poem: The Transactional Theory of Literary Work*. Carbondale: Southern Illinois University.

———. 1985a. "The Transactional Theory of the Literary Work: Implications for Research." In *Researching Response to Literature and the Teaching of Literature*, edited by C. Cooper. Norwood, NJ: Ablex.

———. 1985b. "Viewpoints: Transaction Versus Interaction: A Terminological Rescue Operation." In *Research in the Teaching of English* 19(1): 96–107.

Rumelhart, David E. 1980. "The Building Blocks of Cognition." In *Theoretical Issues in Reading Comprehension: Perspectives from Cognitive Psychology, Linguistics, Artificial Intelligence, and Education*, edited by Rand J. Spiro, Bertram C. Bruce, and William F. Brewer. Hillsdale, NJ: Erlbaum.

Ruzzo, Karen, and Mary Anne Sacco. 2004. *Significant Studies for Second Grade*. Portsmouth, NH: Heinemann.

Scholastic and YouGov. 2014. "Kids and Family Reading Report, 5th Edition." http://www.scholastic.com/readingreport/Scholastic-KidsAndFamilyReadingReport -5thEdition.pdf.

School Library Journal staff. 2016. "SLJ's Average Book Prices for 2016." *School Library Journal*, March 7. www.slj.com/2016/03/research/sljs-average-book-prices-for-2016 /#_.

Serravallo, Jennifer. 2010. *Teaching Reading in Small Groups: Differentiated Instruction for Building Strategic Independent Readers*. Portsmouth, NH: Heinemann.

———. 2015. *The Reading Strategies Book: Your Everything Guide to Developing Skilled Readers*. Portsmouth, NH: Heinemann.

———. 2017. *The Writing Strategies Book: Your Everything Guide to Developing Skilled Writers*. Portsmouth, NH: Heinemann.

Shubitz, Stacey. 2016. *Craft Moves: Lesson Sets for Teaching Writing with Mentor Texts*. Portland, ME: Stenhouse.

Sinclair-Tarr, Stacey, and William Tarr, Jr. 2007. "Using Large-Scale Assessments to Evaluate the Effectiveness of School Library Programs in California." *Phi Delta Kappan* (May): 710–11.

Smith, Aaron. 2015. *U.S. Smartphone Use in 2015*. Washington, DC: Pew Research Center. www.pewinternet.org/2015/04/01/us-smartphone-use-in-2015/.

Smith, Frank. 1988. *Joining the Literacy Club: Further Essays into Education*. Portsmouth, NH: Heinemann.

Swallow, Rick. "Readers Theater." Timeless Teacher Stuff. www.timelessteacher stuff.com.

Szymusiak, Karen, and Franki Sibberson. 2001. *Beyond Leveled Books: Supporting Transitional Readers in Grades 2–5*. Portland, ME: Stenhouse.

Tartt, Donna. 2013. *The Goldfinch*. New York: Little, Brown.

Teresa, Emily C. 2017. *Kids and Family Reading Report*. 6th ed. New York and London: Scholastic and YouGov. www.scholastic.com/readingreport/key-findings .htm#top-nav-scroll.

Thompson, Terry. 2015. *The Construction Zone: Building Scaffolds for Readers and Writers*. Portland, ME: Stenhouse.

Vinton, Vicki. 2017. *Dynamic Teaching for Deeper Reading: Shifting to a Problem-Based Approach*. Portsmouth, NH: Heinemann.

Walker, Rob. 2003. "The Guts of a New Machine." *New York Times Magazine*, November 30. www.nytimes.com/2003/11/30/magazine/the-guts-of-a-new-machine.html.

We Need Diverse Books. n.d. https://diversebooks.org.

Wiggins, Grant. 2012. "Seven Keys to Effective Feedback." *Educational Leadership* 70 (1): 10–16.

Woodson, Jacqueline. 2012. *Each Kindness*. New York: Nancy Paulsen Books.

Worthy, Jo, Megan Moorman, and Margo Turner. 1999. "What Johnny Likes to Read Is Hard to Find in School." *Reading Research Quarterly* 34 (1): 12–27. www.jstor .org/stable/748267?seq=1#page_scan_tab_contents.

Xplore. 2001–17. BrainyQuote.com. www.brainyquote.com/quotes/quotes/a/alex anderg387728.html. Accessed July14, 2107.

Zimmermann, Susan. 2003. *7 Keys to Comprehension: How to Help Your Kids Read It and Get It!* New York: Three Rivers.